DEFEND YOURSELF

A COMPREHENSIVE SECURITY PLAN FOR THE ARMED HOMEOWNER

ROB PINCUS

Published by

Gun Digest® Books, an imprint of F+W Media, Inc.
Krause Publications • 700 East State Street • Iola, WI 54990-0001
715-445-2214 • 888-457-2873
www.krausebooks.com

To order books or other products call toll-free 1-800-258-0929
or visit us online at www.gundigeststore.com

ISBN-13: 978-1-4402-3831-4
ISBN-10: 1-4402-3831-6

Edited by Jennifer L.S. Pearsall
Designed by Jana Tappa
Cover Design by Dave Hauser

Printed in China

ACKNOWLEDGMENTS

In 2012, I was invited to participate in a television show called *Trigger Time*, which was to be sponsored by Crossbreed Holsters and hosted by my good friend Mark Craighead. It was the last project I got to work on with Mark before we lost him. He passed, far too soon, in August 2013, about halfway through the airing of the season. Looking back, I remember that I wasn't terribly excited about the project when I took it on—and now I am forever grateful to both Mark and Troy Guillote, the show's producer, for giving me that opportunity.

ABOUT THE AUTHOR

Rob Pincus, owner, I.C.E. Training Company and creator of the highly respected Combat Focus® Shooting Program, is a professional trainer, author, and consultant. He and his staff at I.C.E. Training Company provide services to military, law enforcement, private security, and students interested in self-defense. Rob provides efficient training methodologies that stress gaining maximum value from limited training resources, as well as methods that work with what the body does naturally under real-world conditions.

Rob has experience as a law enforcement officer and executive protection agent, and he was also commissioned as an officer in the United States Army Reserve after graduating from the Military College of Vermont with a degree in Political Science. He currently serves the San Miguel County Sheriff's Office as a Training Officer and has been a staff writer with *S. W.A. T. Magazine* since 2001.

From 2003 through 2007, Rob was the director of The Valhalla Training Center, in Montrose, Colorado. There he developed the training doctrines and programs that brought Valhalla to the attention of the entire shooting industry as a leading source of reality-based firearms training. Rob was recognized with the Range of the Year award by the National Association of Shooting Ranges, in 2007.

In Late 2007, Rob launched I.C.E. (the letters spoken individually—I-C-E—rather than the word "ice") Training Company and began traveling and teaching around the world. He is one of the busiest instructors in the industry, conducting well over 50 courses a year in more than 40 locations. He travels more than 300 days a year, bringing cutting edge personal-defense information to students ranging from military and law enforcement special operations personnel to those who are just considering their first defensive firearm.

In 2005, Rob began production of the *Personal Defense Firearms* DVD series, which evolved to inclusion in the Personal Defense Network online resource for training information. In addition to his print, video, and in-person teaching, Rob has been involved in the production of several TV shows including *Personal Defense TV, Best Defense, Stop The Threat, World News Tonight, The Daily Show, Best Defense: Survival, Weaponology, Trigger Time,* and dozens of local and regional news pieces covering training and firearms rights and responsibilities topics.

Recently, Rob has focused on program and instructor development. Instructor groups that have sought out his expertise and integrated components of his programs into their own include the Chicago Police Department FTU, South Wales Police Department Training Unit (UK), Naval Special Warfare S.E.A.L. Qualification Training, Bavarian Polizie (Germany), Orange County (Florida) Sheriff's Office, and the 19th Group Army Special Forces. He also conducts an annual conference for certified Combat Focus Shooting Instructors and is one of the founders of the Association of Defensive Shooting Instructors.

INTRODUCTION

The information you are about to read will be most obviously valuable, if you have a firearm for home-defense. Even if you do not, I believe that the information contained here is still important.

If you have not yet made the choice to have a firearm, or several, staged for the defense of your home or family, this information will be instrumental in your decision of whether or not you should. If you do decide to make that choice, the information in this book will guide your purchases, preparation, and training. But even if you never decide to have a home-defense firearm, this information will help you in many other facets of home-defense. This book will be especially important if you have family members you're interested in protecting in a worst-case scenario.

When you're inside your home, you should be safe and secure, but the fact is you may be targeted by someone who wants to hurt you or your family. You may, as so often is told in the news headlines of today, become the victim of a terrible act of violence inside your home. Accepting that fact and preparing to keep it from happening is not only a right, it is your responsibility. By making it harder for violent predators to hurt us and by actively defending ourselves from them, we can reduce the propensity for them to act. By making your home and family safer, you truly contribute to making the world a better place.

—Rob Pincus

FOREWORD

've known Rob Pincus for many years. His is one of the most inquisitive and innovative minds in the firearms and tactics world. I've taken some of his training, and he's taken some of mine—and in this book, I think, he has hit some nails solidly on their heads.

I was at the NRA Annual Meetings in Houston, in 2012, when the mainstream media pounced on Rob. In the course of a lecture on response to home invasion, he included the option of having a gun in a lockbox in your kid's room, so as to allow you and your spouse to run there and arm yourselves, as just one possible option. The anti-gunners in the media went nuts, creating the false implication that Pincus was a crazy man to suggest that loaded guns be left "indiscriminately available" to little children.

Of course, that wasn't what he said, nor something he implied. Rob had quite clearly stated that in this training model, the gun would locked in a safe container, one that *only* the parent could open. It would allow the parents to get to the kids' room to protect them there, and faster than the proposition of the parent liberating the weapon in their own master bedroom first and *then* making their way toward the children's room—and, perhaps, too late. Again, Rob presented this idea as a clearly valid option, but closed minds just couldn't comprehend it.

To get the most from the book you're about to read, you need a practical mind and an open one—something the media clearly lacked during Rob's lecture I attended. Rob explains his explanations in precise detail. Therefore, it will take a detailed reading for you to get the most out of this book.

No two instructors in this business agree 100 percent on everything, and that's certainly true of Rob Pincus and me. At the same time, Rob has, undeniably, put some solid, life-saving advice into this book. The pre-planning he advises will very likely make the difference between life and death, if you are ever in the situation this book was written to address. Give it the careful reading it deserves and you'll better achieve the safety you and your family deserve.

—*Massad Ayoob, August 2013*

About Massad Ayoob: *One of the pre-eminent fighting handgun trainers in the world, Massad Ayoob is the author of* Gun Digest Book of Concealed Carry, Combat Shooting with Massad Ayoob, The Gun Digest Book of Combat Handgunnery, *and several other books (see www. gundigeststore.com for more information and resources). Ayoob is one of the very few Five Gun Masters among the 10,000-member International Defensive Pistol Association, and was the first to earn that title. He served 19 years as chair of the Firearms Committee of the American Society of Law Enforcement Trainers and several years as a member of the Advisory Board of the International Law Enforcement Educators and Trainers Association. In addition to teaching for those groups, he founded the Lethal Force Institute, has taught for the International Association of Law Enforcement Firearms Instructors and International Homicide Investigators, and frequently serves as an expert witness in court cases about shootings and weapons. His "Stress-Fire" method of reflexive, yet accurate shooting at high speed was adopted by the U.S. Army as part of its standard pistol training course. Today, he runs the Massad Ayoob Group, training students everywhere in the art of armed self-defense.*

There are three places a gun owner is most likely to fire their weapon—and two of those places rightfully scare the hell out of most reasonable people.

We fire our weapons at the range in case, God forbid, we have to ever fire them at home or on the street. As responsible gun owners, we value our marksmanship skills. We understand that we train not only to hit what we're shooting at, but also to make sure we don't hit unintended targets. But is this enough?

"Train like you fight and fight like you train" is a popular mantra with military and law enforcement officers, and for good reason. When placed under a highly stressful situation, human beings default to what's natural. In a life or death situation, elevated heart rate, tunnel vision, auditory exclusion, and a host of other involuntary physiological responses are all but guaranteed. As your body's fight-or-flight mechanism kicks in, you'll either freeze on the spot or default to how you have trained yourself to react.

This is more than aligning your gun's sights on your target, calming your breathing, and gently depressing the trigger. Before you even engage a would-be attacker, you have to have already thought through your entire plan of action. If you think you can put that off and just decide how you'll handle things if and when the situation presents itself, you are in for a very rude and potentially deadly awakening.

In addition to the host of moral and legal implications involved with the use of a firearm in a deadly threat or a threat of grievous bodily harm scenario, there is a tsunami of tactical implications. If you hear the glass break while you're in the kitchen, where will you run first? Your children's room? Your own bedroom to retrieve your firearm and then to your children's room? Is your bedroom even the best place to keep your firearm? Can you afford to safely secure a firearm in your children's room? Can you afford not to? What about keeping one in the den? How about another in the kitchen?

From exploring your self-defense options and areas of need to drilling with your family through various self-defense scenarios and dealing with law enforcement before, during, and after an event, this book is packed with years of insight and exceptional tactical detail. Simply put, there are few people who know the art of self-defense like Rob Pincus.

Success in life comes down to having a plan, as well as the courage to execute that plan. When and if the time ever comes, only you can make the decision as to what's right for you and your family. What you *cannot* do is turn back time.

It has been said that firearms are a lot like parachutes. If you ever need one and don't have one, chances are you'll never need one again. If evil ever selects you and those you care about, there won't be any do-overs or mulligans. In a matter of seconds, how you react and whether or not you have a plan of action will make all the difference—for *everyone* involved. Who will the winner be? Will it be you? And what if you kill your attacker? What then?

No responsible human being ever wants to take another person's life. That's not why we arm and train ourselves. We arm and train ourselves so that our lives and the lives of the people we love and care about will never be taken from us or irreparably damaged.

As my mother always told me while I was growing up, "We may not always be able to control the situation we find ourselves in, but we can choose how we will react to it. No one has the right to do harm to you or the people you care about. No one. *Ever*. If your life or the lives of the people you care about are ever threatened, how will you choose to react to it? Will you choose to be prepared? Will you choose to have thought through all the possible scenarios, the appropriate reactions, and the potential consequences? If so, then you will have chosen not to be a victim. This is the book for you. By reading this book, you are demonstrating yourself to be a winner. You are a responsible firearm owner who will never invite evil into your world, but, if it should ever come, you'll be ready to meet it with both the appropriate level of force and a plan that secures yourself and your loved ones.

Firearms are tools. They don't have personalities. They are inanimate objects. It's how they are used that matters. I hope knowing how to use your firearm properly, along with the wisdom in this book, will help you develop a plan that will give you the peace of mind that comes from knowing that, if the time ever comes, you will be as ready as possible to use your firearm to protect not only yourself, but the people who are the most important to you.

Whether you are a seasoned pro or someone completely new to firearms, you will find the information in this book extremely valuable. Read on and enjoy!

—Brad Thor, August 2013

About Brad Thor: *Brad Thor is the author of* Hidden Order, *a No. 1 New York Times best-seller. Other titles include* The Last Patriot, The Lions of Lucerne, Black List, *and* Path of the Assassin. *He is a frequent moderator on the topic of terrorism for such media outlets as FOX News Channel and CNN, he's served as a member of Homeland Security's Analytic Red Cell Unit, and he is a fellow of the Alexandrian Defense Group. To learn more about Brad's writings, visit www.BradThor.com.*

TABLE OF CONTENTS

PART I

HOME INVASION

TACTICS TO SURVIVE

CHAPTER 1

WHAT IS ARMED HOME-DEFENSE?

Protecting your home can take a variety of forms, but adding a firearm to the mix escalates your level of responsibility. Are you ready for that?

Armed home-defense is much more than just shooting an intruder in your home. The shooting act, actually, is just a small part of armed home-defense. In fact, much of your preparation, planning, and action will be geared towards *avoiding* the need to shoot at all!

This concept of avoiding the act of shooting, even though armed in preparation for an event, is *paramount*. First and foremost, you want to avoid confrontation by making your home hard to get into. Even if your home is breached, you still want to avoid violence by evading an attacker, if possible. You should only use force to defend ourselves when confronted with violence.

Armed home-defense simply means that a firearm *plays a role* in your home-defense plan. It is certainly possible to have a home-defense plan that does *not* include a firearm, but it would be a much weaker plan, one that, ultimately, would not afford you the most efficient option for meeting a lethal threat with an equally powerful defense.

Understanding when to use your firearm is an important piece of the puzzle in planning your armed home-defense. The law, certainly, is your starting point and a guide to the ownership and use of a firearm. Laws regarding purchase, storage, and defensive use in your specific location are beyond the purview of this book, due to the myriad variations across states and individual towns and cities, but they are your responsibility to learn and obey. If you're going to make a plan for armed home-defense, in addition to federal laws, your state, region, county, city, or town most likely has its own set of regulations you will need to research.

After you understand the laws, you will need to tackle both the ethical and tactical issues surrounding the use of a firearm. Once you've dealt with whether you will have a firearm for home-defense at all and then decided to venture down that path, you'll need to figure out which one(s) you want to utilize—will your firearm be a handgun, a rifle, or a shotgun? Maybe even a combination of them? Will your firearm(s) be carried with you around the home or will it be stored in a locked safe? As you progress through this book, you'll see that there may be one firearm or many staged around your home as part of your overall home-defense plan.

Armed home-defense is a lot more than just choosing a firearm and learning to shoot. Aside from the firearm itself, if you're taking home-defense seriously, you'll be thinking about locks, doors, windows, floor plans, barricades, training sessions, family discussions, home-defense drills, and many other things. This is a *big* undertaking, one that can leave you overwhelmed with its many facets. The best place to start is with an understanding of the problems you may face and the decisions you ultimately make about how you want to deal with them if you need to. I'll tackle these concepts in the next two chapters.

If, at any point, you start to think that a *complete* home-defense plan is more than you bargained for, don't forget that *any steps you take are better than none.* Even the simple act of reading this book and thinking about the responses you may have to make when encountering a violent incident could save your life in the heat of the moment. Armed

If you're looking down the barrel of a gun, it's too late to start planning for your defense.

Armed home-defense is not an all or nothing proposition. Do what you can, as you can, and you'll be many steps ahead of the average person who doesn't even consider these things.

home-defense is *not* an all or nothing proposition. Do what you can, as you can—everyone has limited training resources, for instance, something I'll cover more in Appendix C—and you'll be many steps ahead of the average person who doesn't consider these things.

The last thing I that I will say in this section is that this book is *not* a fundamental firearms instruction manual. This is a book about home-defense that includes information about and related to the ownership, storage, and use of a firearm, but it is by no means meant to be a complete treatment on the topic of firearms, defensive or otherwise. In addition to the information contained herein, you are encouraged to seek out specific defensive shooting instruction. My preference is to get that training from a certified Defensive Firearms Coach (DFC) or Combat Focus® Shooting Instructor. While there are many sources available for firearms instruction, these are the two types of defensive shooting instructors

that have been certified by my company (www.combatfocusshooting.com; www.icetraining.us). DFCs and CFS Instructors are located all around the United States and Europe. I will add that, as an introduction to basic firearms ownership and shooting principals, you will find no better source than the National Rifle Association (NRA; www.nra.org). The NRA has the largest collection of instructors on the planet, each of whom are certified to teach you the basics. Beyond the basics, ultimately, the live-fire course most aligned with the information contained in this book will be found in I.C.E. Training Company's Introduction to Home-defense Handguns Course, which is taught by the team of DFCs.

Regardless whether you get your training from my business or someone else's, be sure to get proper instruction in the maintenance and operation of any firearm that you own. Safety is first, last, and always.

CHAPTER 2

THE PLAUSIBILITY PRINCIPLE:

DEFINING JUST WHAT IT IS YOU'RE PREPARING FOR

You can take the time to imagine every awful, criminal event that could happen to your home, but, if you try to apply your resources to cover all of them, you'll go insane. **This is how you narrow the field and save your time, resources, and sanity.**

How do you decide how to train and practice? How do you decide which situations to train for in the *first* place? Before you answer those questions, let's look at a few other questions that should be asked and answered first, as you begin the process of preparing for home-defense:

- Should I own a gun for home-defense?
- If yes, what type of gun should I choose?
- What ammunition should I load into my chosen gun?
- What type of holster and storage container should I use?
- Where in the home should I stage my gun?

Next, let's look at some of the questions you need to answer as you start to train with a firearm:

- What distance should I shoot at?
- What target size should I shoot at?
- How many shots should I fire?

These questions are incredibly important and they are the subject of many Internet debates and gun shop conversations all around the country. People hold very strong opinions on these topics; even the top instructors in the world often disagree about the answers to these types of questions. Sometimes these disagreements boil down to advocating what someone subjectively likes or what they are most comfortable with because of prior experience. The best answers to these questions for *you,* on the other hand, may not be obvious, but it is important that you try

to answer them both as accurately as possible, and before you begin investing your limited resources (money, time, access to a range, etc.).

There are two ways that you can come to conclusions with these types of questions: science or philosophy. Let's look at both methods.

The first and best approach is science. Science is based on the collecting, observing, and measuring of facts. If you are able to *objectively* collect information about such things as actual dynamic critical incidents (this is a term you'll see often in this book, so I'll abbreviate it to DCI), that have occurred in homes in your area, the reliability of a specific type of firearm, the performance of specific types of bullet penetrating a human body, or anything else pertinent to addressing a home- or personal-defense situation, you will have a strategic advantage in your decision-making process. Too, if, on your own, you can conduct objective and controlled experiments that help you decide between one holster and another or between one type of gun and another, you should.

One experiment that can be conducted with relative ease is a ballistic gelatin test. Ballistic gelatin is a medium for measuring and examining bullet performance, including penetration and expansion. The protocols for testing bullets in this way are very controlled. The gelatin mixture used (this is not supermarket gelatin), and even the temperature of the block when you shoot it need to be maintained in specific ways, so that accurate comparisons can be made from one bullet to another.

You could also collect data on assaults that occur inside homes in your town

Experiments such as those comparing bullet performance through the use of ballistic gelatin is an important part of the scientific approach to defending one's home.

and determine whether the attackers are most often strangers or people known to the victims. You could determine whether the attackers already had access to the house or if they forced their way in. You could learn what time of the day most of the assaults happened.

Know that after scientific experiments and data collection are done, it is likely you'll still be left with many unanswered questions. There are so many variables in this area of study, you could never perform all the tests and experiments necessary, nor predict the circumstances to a high enough degree of certainty. It would be impossible to *know* that you were making the right choices based on objective facts alone.

At this point, your guide through the decision making process will have to be philosophy. You'll need to apply logic and rational thought to the facts you are able to collect and develop sound conclusions that allow you to make your final decisions. At my I.C.E. Training Company, we use a concept called the "plausibility principle" to guide our thought process regarding exactly what we're going to prepare for, the gear we're going to have with us, and how we're going to prepare for to use that gear and implement our prepared plan.

DEFINING THE POSSIBILITIES

Because your training resources are limited, and because it is highly unlikely you would ever actually face a need to defend yourself from violence in your home, you have to justify the effort you spend on training and preparation. You have to prioritize exactly what it is you are training and buying gear and making plans for. Truly, you cannot even come close to specifically preparing for every conceivable possible threat you could imagine. *Time* to train, *money* to train, *ammunition* to train, and *access* to ranges, classes, and more are all limited to some extent for everyone. So, because everyone's resources are limited, no one is truly able to comprehensively train for every possibility. So where do you start? By training for the things that are most likely.

Take a look at the graphic in this section. The biggest circle represents everything that is *possible*. If you, at this very moment, were to think of every type of attack that could possibly happen

to you at some point in life, you would find yourself with some pretty daunting and extreme situations to get ready for. Imagine that four masked terrorists with assault rifles suddenly broke through every door and window to the building you are in. You would need to surrender, escape, or use force to stop them. How much training, practice, and conditioning do you need? What equipment would you want? Could you modify the house ahead of time to give you an easy escape route or barricade location? Is all of that really worth the expenditure of training resources?

The justification for that expenditure would depend on how likely you believed that type of attack would be. If you absolutely knew that such an attack was coming in three months and you had to get ready, it would be pretty easy to justify. But you just can't know such a thing— and the chances of it ever happening are, actually, incredibly remote. It is *possible*, but it's not very *probable*.

A lot of people get quickly overwhelmed, when they start thinking about everything that's possible. What they really need to think about are the situations that are most probable. Once you are secure in the answer to that questions, then you need to spend most of your time training for what is most likely to happen, because that is how you will be able to most efficiently use your limited resources.

Remember, it's not *highly likely* you're ever going to need to use a gun to defend yourself or anyone else. It is not *highly likely* that your home will ever be invaded by violent predators. It is not *probable* you will need to use force of any kind to

THE PLAUSIBILITY PRINCIPLE

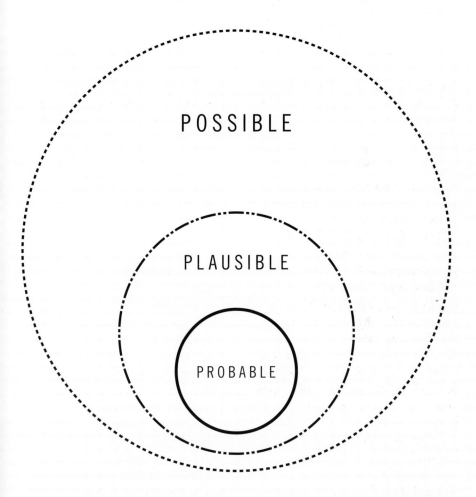

This diagram can help you take the dizzying and overwhelming array of what *could* happen to you and reduce it down to the scenarios *most likely* to happen. Could a local gang faction decide to invade your home and take it for their own turf? Sure, but that's not likely. Better to think about and prepare for defending you and yours against something much more realistic, like the average bad guy looking for an easy home to rob.

If you're going to take home-defense seriously, it's those situations that are the most probable that become the ones for which you must prepare.

defend yourself on any given day, but any of these situations is *possible*. The fact that you are reading this book indicates that you have accepted that the possibility of needing to defend yourself and your family in your home is high enough to warrant your attention. Your acceptance of this *possibility* is what justifies the amount of time, effort, and energy you commit to training. You've crossed the mental line from and acknowledged the appropriateness and wisdom of preparing for armed home-defense.

This choice is probably not one you made lightly. Still, for some of you reading this book, you remain unsure about just how many resources you're willing to devote to this endeavor. Whenever you are making a choice to train, purchase equipment, or modify your home, think about how plausible it is that you will both need and be able to use your newly acquired defensive assets.

FROM POSSIBILITIES DERIVE PROBABILITIES

Now that you've crossed that line, you need to identify the most *probable* circumstances under which you would be forced to defend yourself. That's what the smallest circle in the graphic represents, the most likely scenarios you would face in a home-defense situation. If you are going to take home-defense seriously,

this area and its scenarios are the ones for which you must prepare.

Initially, your monthly budget allotment for home-defense may get spent on the most obvious things: new locks, a quality defensive firearm and a quick-access safe, ammunition for practice, tuition for a training course, etc. At some point, however, you will find that you have spent all the money you really *needed* to spend for the probable events. So what do you do with your budget next month? How will you spend it?

This is the gray area that varies from person to person. In the graphic, it is the area labeled "plausible." Plausibility can be thought of as "reasonableness," i.e., how reasonable is it to spend money or time or effort on a certain thing? The reason this is a gray area is that only *your* resources and circumstances will dictate what is reasonable for *you*. For example, for some people, it will be reasonable to have more than one defensive firearm. For others, maybe those with a small budget and a small home, buying multiple firearms might be a waste of resources. For still others, installing a new door might become a priority when there are extra funds, while some would put an alarm system at the top of their list. While this book offers many ways for you to prepare, only you can decide which steps are reasonable to take. The plausibility principle should be your guide.

CHAPTER 3

HOME INVASION:

FIVE FUNDAMENTAL SURVIVAL TACTICS

When it happens to the little old lady a block over from your house, you realize it can really happen to you, too. **Are you prepared to make it through one of the most terrifying events to happen to you in your own home?**

As you begin to think about defending your home, it is important to identify how your preparation, plans, and techniques will actually help you in the worst-case scenario. Understanding what you are preparing for is necessary, in order to develop a plan. There are many scenarios we could prepare for, but I'm going to focus on the one that most people are most scared of, the one that makes the headlines, and the one that gets the attention of even the most complacent person: *home invasion*. A home invasion is a terrifying prospect, one where one or more armed predators intent on hurting you and your family force their way into your home *when they know you are present*. This crime will be a violent, sudden attack—it is an ambush—and it occurs in the place where you should feel (and be) most secure: your home.

In order to deal with this kind of violent, surprise attack, you need to have a well-planned response, and that planned response needs to have been rehearsed. If you do not have a plan, haven't practiced your plan, or your plan is overly complicated, you will be left with nothing more than hope and the possibility of improvisation. You'll be counting on luck or the mercy of your attackers to get you through the situation—and neither is a high-value proposition.

As we talk about preparing for an imminent home invasion, you'll find that many of the preparations you make to defend yourself in such a situation will also help you in virtually every other critical incident: burglary, robbery, attack inside your home, betrayal and assault from someone you trusted, etc. Even

If escape isn't an option, get a barrier between you (and your family) and the bad guys. A reinforced door is the preferable first choice (and pushing some heavy furniture up against one often isn't a bad idea, either).

your readiness for threats like fire, some natural disasters, and civil unrest will be enhanced through your efforts to be ready for a violent surprise invasion. In other words, once you take responsibility for your own defense and you start thinking *proactively*, your safety will be increased in all ways.

The following five steps comprise the basis for the title of this chapter, the fundamental tactics of home-defense. Understanding them is vital to forming a plan, training to execute that plan, and completing every other preparation you will make for armed home-defense. This is the most important section of this book.

EVADE

If you can get away from a violent situation, do it. While it may seem noble and brave to think that you should stand up to anyone who dares to enter your home, meet them at the earliest possible point, and deal with them swiftly to deliver the justice they deserve, you need to remember that your stuff, your things, are not worth dying for. You do not live in an action movie—the aftermath of a defensive shooting lasts forever.

Evasion is the first home-defense tactic, because it is the one that trumps the efforts of the bad guy to hurt you. If you are not present, you aren't going to get hurt. Your stuff may get stolen, your home and belongings may be damaged, but you can replace stuff and you can repair houses and things. You can't get un-killed. You can't get un-raped. You also can't be sure you'll avoid criminal charges or civil court proceedings, if you shoot a home intruder. All around, much better to avoid the situation, if you can.

We define "evasion" as getting away from an attacker or out of range of the attack. How and when you evade is important. So, how do you evade an attacker? There are lots of ways, you just have to think through them. For instance, evasion may mean that you run out the front door and go to a neighbor's house, when you discover someone trying to surreptitiously enter your home through the back door. Evasion may mean that you move from the first floor of your home to the second floor after discovering an intruder. Again, you have to do the work of thinking through possible situations and identifying how you'll get away. Still, there are some rules to making your plans.

First, you should never evade if doing so actually puts you in *more* danger. If you are facing an attacker with a knife and you will *not* be able to move safely to another room or behind a barricade of some type, you will need to stand and defend yourself. Turning your back on an armed attacker who is already moving in a close space is a recipe for disaster. Similarly, if you are on the second floor and you would have to jump out of a window to get away from a threat, it would likely be foolish to expose yourself to the known danger of getting hurt when you land—especially knowing that, if you were injured in our landing, you would then likely be caught by your attacker anyway.

The second rule is to never leave your family behind. While this may seem self-evident, it needs to be written down and printed in this book and you need to read it. I wouldn't want anyone to read this book and mistakenly think that I am advising you to leave your spouse, parents, children, or anyone else to fend for themselves as you escape harm. I also wouldn't want anyone to try to use the omission of this point against you in court (or otherwise). Stick together with your family. Work together to defend yourselves, whenever possible. Of course, you should also attempt to gather everyone together and evade as a group, if possible.

The third rule is to move only into a known area when possible, but not into one with more potential danger. Don't run outside of your home without attempting to make sure that outside is clear of potential threats. Say you find someone trying to enter your home through one door. You may want to flee out the front, but you don't know if the person breaking in the back is acting alone. There just may be the threat of someone watching the opposite entry and, in such a situation, you are probably better off staying put and using other defensive tactics in your home than you would be running outside and into a confrontation with a violent predator on neutral ground.

BARRICADE

If you can't get away, your next step should be to try to barricade yourself. We define "barricade" as making it harder for the attacker to reach you.

Barricading doesn't have to mean locking yourself and your family into a vault that you've had built in the center of your home. In fact, it may just simply mean closing a door and being quiet enough so that the bad guy never finds you. Barricading could mean improvis-

ing a barrier, such as a piece of furniture against a door, or it could mean positioning yourself in a remote part of the home in a corner of a room. Regardless your level of barricade, the best barricade situation will take advantage of reinforced doors and other preparations that you have set up ahead of time.

At this point, the term "hide" is very appropriate. "Hiding" is a combination of evasion and barricading. If you keep the definitions of both tactics in mind, you'll realize that you could simply duck down behind a piece of furniture in the dark, stay quiet, and avoid contact and be successfully completing both evasion and barricading.

When you're choosing (or planning) a barricade point, there are some things you should keep in mind.

First, put as many doors and corners as possible between you and the known position of the intruder or their most likely entry points.

Second, do not hide in a closet. If you have the time to put yourself in a position of advantage, give yourself some standoff distance for response time and decision making between you and the last door/corner. Not only do you want to stay outside of arm's reach of a threat whenever possible, you may also have police, neighbors, or an unaccounted for family member coming towards you, and putting some space between you and them gives you more time to make the correct shoot or don't-shoot decision.

Third, if you can, set yourself up at a 90-degree angle off the line of travel that any approaching threat would be taking. This will give you the maximum advantage in your response to any threat and, again, enhance your ability to identify who is coming towards you.

ARM

In the event that you need to respond directly to a threat inside your home, obviously, you want to have every advantage possible. It has been said that a firearm is a "great equalizer." Your size, strength, and other physical factors are much less of an issue, when you hold the power of a defensive weapon *and have the skill to use it.*

That last bit is the trick, of course. While a firearm certainly does increase your defensive capabilities, your physical attributes still play a factor in all aspects of personal-defense. If all you do is only put a gun in your hand and nothing else, I think you are stretching the concept of "armed." In fact, being armed may not have anything to do with a firearm. Certainly, you're going to want some sort of tool, though, and a firearm is indeed a great tool to have.

When I teach home-defense, I sometimes change the order in which I explain "arm" and "barricade." Why? For the average person not taking significant steps ahead of time to prepare for their defense, the idea of establishing a barricade in the heat of the moment is more far-fetched. Therefore, I often talk to people about arming themselves before I mention barricading, because, if you find yourself with an intruder in your immediate presence, *anything* can become a defensive tool.

Given that you are reading this book and at least beginning to formulate a home-defense plan, here are some things to keep in mind:

Yes, a baseball bat can be a worthwhile item to have stashed in your home, in the event you cannot get to or for some reason choose not to use your firearm. Like all other such objects you might entertain for inclusion in your home-defense plan, you need to consider where and how you position it for your access or access by your family members, and not possession by the bad guy.

First, anything can be a defensive tool, if employed as such. Start looking around the room you are in right now and recognize the obvious objects:

- Long objects that can be used as clubs.

- Heavy items than can be used as impact tools (depending on your strength).
- Objects that can be used as a shield, if the attacker has a knife or other contact weapon.
- Edged objects that can be used as a

A simple pocket knife, a kitchen knife, a poker from the fireplace, the barbells you use in your home workout, a piece of furniture, even a heavy book or your sharp-edged tablet, all can be used as defensive tools if needed and if planned for appropriately.

cutting tool (including the obvious kitchen knives and scissors).

Next, start looking at the *least* obvious items in the room you're in—books, blankets, pillows, magazines, cords, bags, shoes. How could they be used as defensive tools to strike, cut, block, or smother an attacker?

Now, as you're beginning to make your plan, think about staging specific defensive tools in places that make the

most sense. Start with your planned barricade area or the place in the house where you spend the most time. (Staging firearms in the home will get a chapter of its own later in the book.)

COMMUNICATE

Communication as it relates to home-defense has two facets: contacting the police and communicating with a home intruder. We'll cover the latter first.

Communicating with the intruder might keep you from having to shoot, but I do *not* recommend that you call out unless you are 100-percent sure your intruder already knows exactly where you are. If you have already been located, if the attacker is trying to break through your last doorway and is threatening you, for example, then, yes, it may be a good idea to communicate. If, on the other hand, your intruder doesn't know your location, you don't want to give away your position or attract attention by calling out a warning meant to let your intruder know that you are armed and will defend yourself.

While you may feel that it is morally appropriate to call out a warning, that is absolutely *not* why I am recommending against it. Communicating with the attacker, specifically letting him know that you are prepared to defend yourself and that the police are on the way, is a tactic that may cause a psychological stop to that intruder. But the chance of your threat choosing to avoid confrontation at the last minute or trying to flee before the police arrive is not worth exposing

yourself to extra risk, and that is why I do not recommend calling out unless you know that contact is imminent anyway.

The second facet of communication is to contact the police. We will cover dealing with the police arriving at your home in detail later in the book. For now, know that you should definitely call the police if you have the opportunity after you have barricaded yourself. The most obvious way to contact the police is by phone. When you call, you'll be talking to a middleman in the emergency services process who needs to know certain things:

- Where you are (address for dispatching of police).
- What's going on.
- That you are armed (if true).
- Attacker description (if possible).
- Your description.

RESPOND

Ultimately, you may need to fight to defend yourself and your family. Take away everything else and you are left to use whatever force is necessary to stop the threat. The fight could take many forms, but we will assume that the use of a firearm will be appropriate, hence the focus on armed home-defense. Whether the other tactics fail or you simply never have an opportunity to employ them doesn't matter. Because you can't really predict the exact circumstances you will face, it is imperative that you prepare for the worst-case scenario, knowing that you can deal with lesser threats with less effort.

5 FUNDAMENTAL SURVIVAL TACTICS

1 EVADE

2 BARRICADE

3 ARM

4 COMMUNICATE

5 RESPOND

CHAPTER 4

THE BEST-LAID PLANS

(FLEXIBILITY REQUIRED)

A problem in your home will be an elastic event—
changing, shifting, unpredictable.
Your pre-problem planning can help keep you in control.

Fundamental home-defense tactics do not need to be deployed linearly, i.e., in a specific order. Indeed, you may find yourself acting outside of a planned order or even cycling through various tactics during the duration of an incident. Let's look at a couple examples.

Let's say you see an intruder in your backyard and notice that your deadbolt isn't locked, so your first move is to barricade by locking the bolt. Next you might evade to an upstairs bedroom, where you employ a mechanical bar-ricade on the door, arm yourself with a rifle, and use a cell phone to communicate with the police. Now let's say the bad guy runs towards the door and bursts through it as you were trying to employ the deadbolt. In that case, you might need to jump straight to responding with physical force, knocking him down as he enters and then evading by running through the house and out an opposite door to a neighbor's home, where you could communicate with the police.

Cooking dinner, you spy a stranger in your backyard, jiggling the door on your locked tool shed. One of your first moves might be to throw the deadbolt on your main entry doors, but you have to think through that scenario and plan that action around the cue to have it work when the situation's real.

The point of painting such pictures is to prevent you from thinking that you cannot do exactly what is most appropriate or necessary at any given moment. The very nature of training to be efficient demands that you be fluid, rather than locked into some pre-determined "master plan."

As you begin to devise plans and options to deal with various threats, you will want to set cues in place. These precursor cues should become stimuli that elicit your responses. For instance, one of the things I learned while working on the first season of Outdoor Channel's *The Best Defense: Survival* was how people who live in flood risk areas plan actions based on cues they've setup and taken from rising water levels. People who live near rivers with flood histories have learned that they need to set in place actual physical markers—posts, large rocks, etc.—to cue them to take certain actions. One marker might prompt them to remove items from a basement, while another would tell them to secure items from the first floor. Moving up the chain of risk, other cues would tell when to pack a bag, stage irreplaceable items in their home or remove them for the area, and, finally, when they should evacuate. By setting these markers, residents near those flood-prone areas avoid needing to make decisions under pressure and emotional distraction. They also avoid rationalizing inaction in the face of possible threat, and they avoid needing to improvise, because they have an actionable plan already in place.

Let's take the above example and apply it to the lessons here. Precursor cues for home-defense could be based on time of day (when to set an alarm), activities in your community (when to use perimeter lighting), a change in relationship status (when to change your locks or security alarm codes), actions from your dog (when to barricade), and actions or words from someone inside your home (when to ask them to leave), or at the door (when to call the police). As you can see, there are many things you need to consider as you think about deploying the fundamentals of home-defense.

CHAPTER 5

THE DYNAMIC CRITICAL INCIDENT:
(SURPRISE!)

You can plan out your responses to a possible intruder in your home a hundred different ways—and you should—but, when it actually happens, you also need to be prepared for those plans to go to hell.

Welcome to chaos.

f you are interested in armed home-defense, you must accept the possibility of being in a situation where you can't choreograph your response. You need to train and plan in a way that deals with the reality of the attack catching you off-guard. We call that moment the "dynamic critical incident." Dynamic critical incident (DCI) is the fancy phrase for our home-defense event, but it's also very specific terminology that means a very specific thing.

DCI's have three components: they are *surprising*, they are *chaotic*, and they are *threatening*. If we're talking about defensive firearms training, then there is also specifically a *threat* to which the most appropriate response is active defense, possibly including a firearm.

"Surprising" simply means that you didn't know the event was going to happen. If you knew it was going to happen, of course, you might have avoided it. You wouldn't have opened the front door, for example, if you knew you were about to be robbed by the person on your porch. If you knew there were two armed punks waiting for you to turn off the TV and go to bed, you wouldn't forget to set the security alarm. If you knew that your plumber was a rapist, you wouldn't have been home alone while he was working on your sink. Of course, you also certainly wouldn't be likely to hire a plumber who was a rapist if you knew that about him, but you need to be open to the idea that the one you do hire might be.

That isn't paranoia, that's part of understanding that, at the extreme, a home attack has absolutely no warning and is a complete surprise. Say the plumber looked at you oddly and gave you a weird feeling when he was at the house to provide you an estimate and that feeling caused you to invite a friend over to the house when he was scheduled to come back. Such actions mean you would be safer and you would be more prepared. Even if he did attack, you would be more primed for response and more likely to perform the tactics and techniques that you had trained for, because you were not completely surprised.

"Chaotic" means you don't know what's going to happen next. There are lots of events that are initially surprising in this context, but many events that start out in a surprising manner then become very predictable. Chaotic situations, on the other hand, have no rhyme or reason. In chaotic situations, from one second to the next, you must be processing information and adapting to the changing circumstances.

These types of events largely undermine the possibility of a pre-programed, choreographed response. Certainly, there are aspects of our training that are highly planned and practiced precisely—experienced shooters, for instance, would know how to perform a slide-lock reload—but these things are small parts of the bigger picture of a DCI. While you are applying your practiced skills (presentation from the holster, recoil management, deviation control, etc.), as planned, the world around you is changing, responding, and adapting in ways that you cannot predict specifically and yet will need to keep up with. It is for this reason that you must learn your skills at an incredibly automated level. This requires choosing skills that are intuitive (i.e., work well with what the body does naturally), and training for them in the context of the fight.

The definition of "threatening" might seem pretty obvious, but it is important to remember that, in this book, we are specifically talking about a threat to which the appropriate response is going to be the use of lethal force facilitated by reaching for, presenting, and shooting your defensive firearm. That said, it is important to understand two things. First, not all threats to you or those you care about should be responded to with a firearm. Second, reaching for a gun is not always the best thing to do, even when you are in a dynamic critical incident against someone attacking you with lethal force. Certainly, you can (and should!) approach your training for non-firearms situations from a counter-ambush perspective, as well. Although much of the information in this book is clearly directed at defending yourself with a handgun, the biggest and most important concepts can be applied to any aspect of preparation to defend yourself from harm.

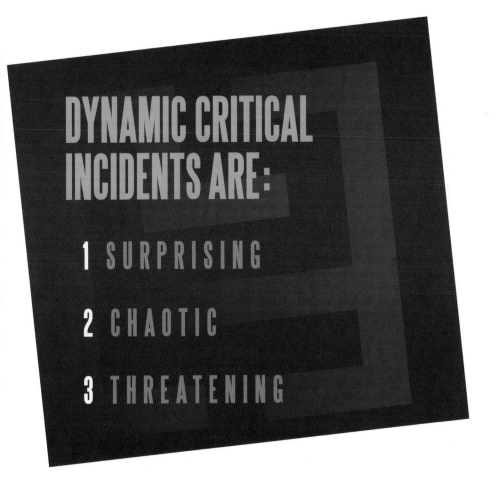

DYNAMIC CRITICAL INCIDENTS ARE:

1 SURPRISING

2 CHAOTIC

3 THREATENING

CHAPTER 6

EVERY GUN IN ITS PLACE:
STAGING DEFENSIVE FIREARMS

Stashing a gun in the right place in order to deal with a threat in the home takes careful thinking and, sometimes, imagination. (Hint: it's not your padded gun case.)

O nce you've made the decision to have a firearm in your home for the defense of yourself or your family in a worst case-scenario, one of the first things you have to deal with is where and how you're going to stage that firearm.

First, you need to determine *how* you will store a firearm in the home. Are you going to keep it secured? Are you going to keep it in a safe? Or do you not have to worry about unauthorized access to your firearm inside your home, because maybe there aren't kids or the kids have been trained to be responsible and trusted firearms owners? Do you live alone or with others? Do you live in a place where laws dictate how you must store your firearms and/or ammunition? After you have met any legal obligations where you

live, staging a firearm for home-defense becomes a balance between accessibility and prevention of unauthorized access.

UNAUTHORIZED ACCESS

"Unauthorized access" is any access to the firearm by those not specifically permitted by you as a responsible firearms owner. This could be someone untrained in firearms, someone trained but whom you do not trust with firearms or, obviously, a criminal who intends to steal your firearm or hurt you with it.

Securing a firearm from unauthorized access involving people whom you allow into your home may be harder than securing the firearms from intruders! When you're thinking about keeping your firearms from an intruder, you have many extra layers of physical security and

Soft cases are probably some of the worst places to stage a gun. They do little to prevent unauthorized access, and almost everyone both good and bad knows on sight what they contain.

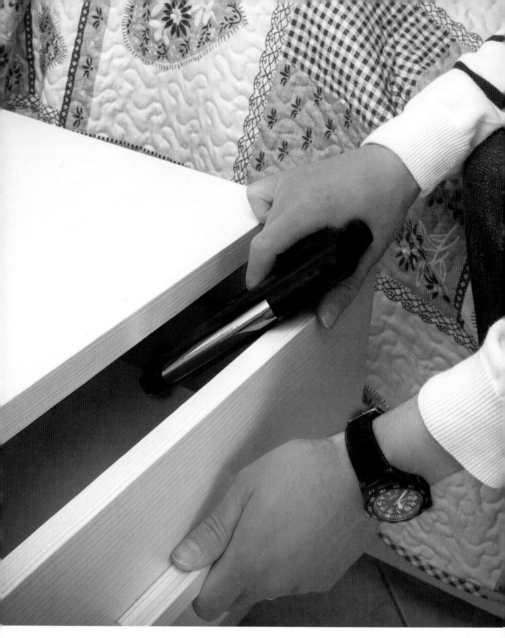

Hiding a gun in a nightstand and otherwise unsecured might be a logical choice if you live by yourself. But remember that this is one of the first places a burglar will look for items when you're not at home, so this kind of staging might be something that becomes part of your nightly routine for you when you go to bed, or even right when you come home from work and you've been carrying your gun on your person all day. Create your home-defense plan according to how you live your life. Make something like taking your gun from your daytime carry holster and putting it in your nightstand an ingrained habit, so that you positively know where your gun is when you need it, and practice accessing it. Consistency is the key to success.

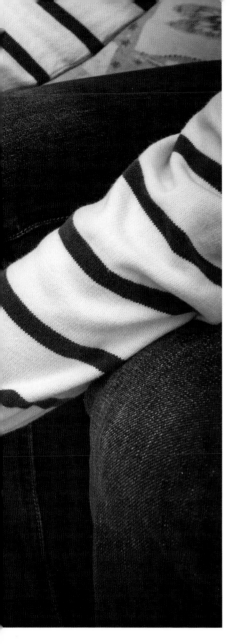

pressures of time and its consequences working in your favor. When it comes to a curious roommate or an undisciplined child, they likely have much more time and access to your storage location. For someone who believes you trust and care for them, there may also be a much lower perception of consequences, should they get caught. At least a thief has real reason to fear getting caught in the act! An unruly child or curious roommate, though, may believe you really won't care or won't really do anything if you find out they were accessing your firearms without permission.

Unless you live alone, the issues surrounding trusted people who aren't authorized to access firearms must be factored into your decision about how to stage those firearms. Even if you do live alone, you still have people you allow into your home from time to time, including guests and service personnel. Most people would agree that simply leaving your firearms loaded and lying around in the open is a mistake. I am also of the opinion that, if you store your firearms and ammunition in two distinctly different locations in your home, you will be hard-pressed to consider them available for home-defense in a dynamic surprise attack.

STAGING VS. STORAGE

Simply keeping a firearm in a soft gun case or plastic rifle case might be one of the worst things you could do with a home-defense firearm. Placing a gun inside of one of these containers does little or nothing to secure them from unauthorized access. Since most people will recognize such containers for exactly what they are, they can't even be said to be hiding the guns. A metal rifle or handgun case may be lockable and offer slightly more security, but, if they are, the locks are inevitably of the fine motor, combination or small key variety and not a great choice for a firearm that may need to be accessed quickly.

I tell you these things because *staging* is different from *storage*. Storage is a possibly long-term solution for guns that you are not planning on using—at all. If you are thinking that a gun may be used for home-defense, then you must stage it. If you have, for instance, a combination safe or one with a key lock, or a safe that has small buttons that need to be pushed, it is hard to consider such a unit appropriate for home-defense.

A heavy-duty safe is great for storage and certainly makes unauthorized access difficult, but it takes time for even the rightful owner to access, thus making it a less than desirable choice for staging.

Mechanical or keyed locks may be mandated by law where you live. You'll have to balance such requirements against how and where you stage your firearms, and you'll need dedicated practice in undoing such devices and getting your gun loaded in a timely manner. Best said, if such locks aren't required (and not otherwise needed), your guns are best staged without them.

Need another example? If you're familiar with handgun holsters, picture an old canvas flap holster from World War II, the type that requires several steps to remove the gun and one that would be very hard to conceal. Storing a home-defense gun in a large combination safe would be the equivalent of choosing that holster for your concealed carry defensive handgun. Could it work? Of course, but that doesn't make it a good idea for someone who is serious about their home-defense planning.

Other, less optimal choices for securing a home-defense gun include trigger locks and cable locks. While these devices can prevent unauthorized people from loading and firing a gun, they are relatively slow and clumsy to remove, require extraneous fine motor skill activity during your chaotic incident, and do nothing to secure your firearm from theft. Too, with enough time and access, these types of locks are easily defeated.

When it comes to securing a staged home-defense firearm, my bottom line best practice recommendation is always going to be a quick-access safe. These kinds of safes are made by many companies and so are of varying quality and efficiency. I have recommended GunVault products for many years. I have tested these safes extensively and find them to be the highest quality and most reliable safes of their kind. In the interest of full disclosure, in 2013, I did agree to be a spokesperson for this company, and for

A quick-access gun safe is a top choice for staging guns that also need to be kept away from unauthorized access. They still need practice accessing them quickly, but such devices equipped with either push-button cypher combination locks or biometric locks (fingerprint recognition) are light years faster to access than cable locks or floor safes.

many years, GunVault has been a sponsor of the *Personal Defense Network*, of which I am the Managing Editor. That said, both those relationships exist because I have been a fan of GunVault's products and recommended them for much longer than I have done business with the company—it's important to understand which came first.

Regardless the brand you choose, a quick-access safe, with either large buttons and a relatively simple/short combination sequence that you can remember or equipped with a reliable biometric scanner, is an outstanding investment for a home-defense gun. Most models are designed for handguns only, but a few will accommodate a shotgun or rifle.

LOADED VS. UNLOADED

The last consideration you will have to make about staging your firearm is whether to keep it loaded. Unless you're talking about a revolver, there's also the related consideration of whether you're going to have a round chambered in the action of the gun, ready to be fired. This is a crucial decision and one that may not have as obvious an answer as you think.

On the one hand, some may say you should *never* have a gun loaded that isn't in your immediate control. Others might say that you should *always* have your defensive guns loaded and ready, otherwise they are useless.

"Always" and "never" are big words. I try to avoid them. As I've mentioned,

This is one of GunVault's biometric handgun safes. Using fingerprint recognition, it is extremely fast to access—for the right person. These compact units fit nicely in a number of places you might want to stage a gun, say, for instance, your kitchen silverware drawer.

there may be laws that govern how you can store firearms and ammunition where you live—those laws must be a guiding force in your decision. Beyond such laws, how you secure your firearms would most likely be the next most important factor, when considering keeping your firearm loaded or unloaded. If you have your firearms locked in a quick-access safe, having them loaded may be just fine. If your defensive firearms aren't secured, though, you really have to pause before you decide to keep them loaded and chambered. Who has access to your home? Who *might* get access to these firearms? You also have to think about the scenarios in which you're going to have a chance to use your staged defensive firearm and see how

much advantage having them loaded and chambered really gives you.

That last bit is important, so let's look at how much time it actually takes to load your defensive firearm and how much time it takes to chamber a round.

If you have a semi-automatic rifle or pistol, it should take you less than two second to insert a magazine and chamber a round. If you double that due to stress, distraction, etc., you are still at only four seconds. If you have the magazine already inserted, it should take you about a second, at the most, to chamber a round once your hand is on the gun—and you can do that while you're bringing the gun to your ready position or even while moving it to a shooting position. There

With practice, loading a double-barreled shotgun is a relatively fast and easy process, but the technique takes time and patience to master correctly.

are many people who advocate *carrying* a gun without a round in the chamber. While I certainly don't agree with them, they do regularly demonstrate just how quickly even an gun lacking a round in the chamber can be brought into action by anyone who practices the technique.

Naturally, if you are using a pump or semi-automatic shotgun or a lever-action rifle, the times would be about the same to chamber, but it takes much longer overall to load such firearms. Loading a double-barreled shotgun can be done quickly (just look at what the Cowboy Action competition shooters do!), but that's a harder skill to acquire than loading a magazine into a semi-automatic handgun.

Let's look at the likely scenarios where you can use a staged home-defense firearm during an incident. It will need to be a scenario where you have time to get to the gun and get it to a ready position and/or an extended shooting position. Why? As you continue reading this book, you will find that things change dramatically when you are within "two arms' reach" of an assailant. In those scenarios, even when you are carrying a gun, I don't recommend going to that gun as your immediate defensive option. Using unarmed skills or simply fighting to get control of your attacker's weapon should be a priority over trying to draw a gun (much less pull one out of a staged location), when someone is actively trying to hurt you and in such a close proximity to do so. In other words, if you can picture yourself running through the house with the bad guy right on your heels and doing some kind of dive-roll onto your gun box, opening it while rolling across the floor, and then coming up to a kneeling position with the gun in your hand just in time to shoot the threat right between the eyes, just as he's about to stick you with a knife … . Well, um, let's reframe that.

If the bad guy is hot on your heels with a knife, you should probably be fighting. Getting stabbed in the back doesn't seem like a good idea and, if the bad guy was strong, smart, and fast enough to get into your home and be posing this kind of direct threat, there is no reason to assume you are suddenly going to be able to outrun him. Even if you can outrun the threat, when you actually get to your gun, there is going to be some amount of time needed to permit you enough control to actually get your gun into your hand, orient it towards the bad guy (preferably at extension), and fire it. It should be obvious, looking at the big picture, that you'd be much better off using some portion of time to barricade yourself, if you can.

If you are reading this book in order to put together a feasible plan of action and you can set up a defensible position with a staged defensive firearm, you should think about including a deadbolt on the door of the room where you have your firearm staged. It takes very little time to slam a door and turn a lock. Taking that amount of time gives you more time to get into position, ready your gun, and prepare for the attacker to break through your barricade. If the attacker can't instantly smash through your reinforced door, you might even be able to make a call to the police to start them on the way. If the threat *is* actively trying to break through the door, you can also let

It should take you less than two seconds to insert a magazine into an empty pistol and chamber a round. Even with stress, that time shouldn't more than double to four seconds. Can you perform this skill that quickly? If not, you have some practicing to do.

them know that you are armed and ready to defend yourself.

A much better scenario for armed home-defense would put you in the location of your staged firearm before the threat was with you. Granted, you can't assume that you'll be fighting on our own terms, but you can do things to make it as hard as possible for a threat to reach you, things like physical home security, being cautious about who you let into your home, and having a response plan ahead of time and enacting it when your precursor cues appear. All those things will set you up for the best possible fight, if and when you need to actively defend yourself with a firearm. They will also do much to buy you that extra one or two seconds needed to load and/or chamber a round if you have chosen to store your gun unloaded or are required to store your firearms that way by law. Ultimately, and when legal, it may be an excellent idea to leave your firearm loaded but without a

When planning for home-defense, it might be wise to consider staging a handgun in—yes, in!—or near the couch.

round in the chamber, or even staged with the magazine removed, though with the gun. Doing so will ensure that you have done a few things once the gun is in your hand:

- It will mean that you must actuate the firearm's slide and have it gripped securely in your hand before you try to use it.
- It will ensure that you aren't foregoing a better defensive option, when the attacker is already touching you or within reach.
- It will mean that you are going to be ensuring that the gun is ready to be used *when you get it into your hand*, as opposed to hoping it was already loaded and being tragically mistaken about its condition. (This may not seem like an issue, but, if you have more that one person using/staging the guns in your home or if you sometimes leave your gun staged and other times have it stored,

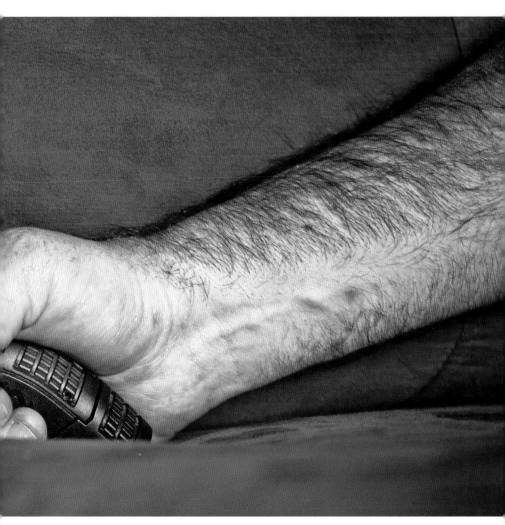

mistakes can be made, especially during times of stress!)

If your firearm is secured in any type of locked container, I see nothing wrong with keeping it loaded and ready, so long as *everyone* with access to the firearm knows that it is in that condition. If you are staging your defensive firearm(s) in a safe with other guns and those other guns are not all loaded, I suggest having a way of distinguishing one set from the other. Perhaps all the non-staged guns can be in soft cases inside the safe. Or maybe your defensive gun(s) will be alone on one side or on one shelf. Some gun safes even come with specific pouches, straps, or sections marked for loaded/defensive firearms.

Outside specific laws, whether you decide to keep your home-defense firearms loaded is going to be your decision. This is an area where there is no solid right or wrong. I have done both, depending on the circumstances I was living in at the time. While you cannot deny the slight advantage to having your guns loaded, there is definitely a much higher risk level with them, if you cannot absolutely control access to them.

My final word on this topic will be one of warning against complacency. Regardless whether you *believe* your guns to be loaded or unloaded *always check them* to be sure that they are actually unloaded when you need them to

Bedside holsters, like this one by Blackhawk!, are a top option for bedroom firearm staging.

be. Treat every gun as if it were loaded, all the time, every time.

STAGING LOCATIONS

Once you have decided *how* to stage your defensive gun, you need to decide *where* you will place them. (There are a lot of options to where you will store a firearm, as well.) If you have multiple firearms, you might even be able to stage firearms in multiple places in your home. You must consider your emergency plan, your tactics, and the viability of being able to use the firearm at all, all in a variety of circumstances. You need to consider the layout of your home, the likely movements of an attacker, and the likely places you're going to be.

Picture yourself inside your home and think about the places you spend most of your time. If you work at home, it may be your office. If you work outside the home, have kids busy with activities, or you have an active social life, most of your home time might be spent asleep in your bedroom. Some people spend a significant amount of time in the living room or den in the evenings. When I've talked to students about this, one area that always seems to come up is the kitchen—and it's worth noting that most kitchens are near at least one outside entrance to the home.

The kitchen may actually be a great place to stage a firearm. If you are in your kitchen and you see an intruder entering (or about to enter) your home, having a firearm staged in a drawer in a quick-access safe would give you the ability to respond immediately to a threat. This would be particularly true, if you have family inside the home and you would not, therefore, be inclined to

evade to another area to retrieve a defensive tool for fear of leaving your family exposed.

Okay, let's say you don't cook. If you spend a lot of time sitting on a couch watching television or playing video games, you'll probably want to consider having a firearm close by there, possibly so close that you don't need to get up from the couch. As cliché as it may seem, a pistol, rifle, or shotgun hidden in the couch cushions might be a viable option for you. Keep in mind that *hiding* a firearm is a valid form of security, if you are taking other appropriate precautions to control access to the areas where the firearm is hidden. If you're going to keep firearms unsecured in such a manner inside of your home, especially if they are loaded, you need to make sure that's legal in the area in which you live. You need to make sure that you're responsible for whomever has access to your home in general, not just to the actual firearms themselves, because anyone who can get into your home *absolutely* has access to that firearm stuffed under the couch cushions. It is beyond the scope of responsible firearms ownership to simply say "I didn't think they'd look in there." History tells us that they will—sometimes with tragic results.

Here's something to consider that a lot of people don't think of: keeping a firearm staged in your child's room. When this information has been misrepresented, I've taken some heat for recommending it in the past, but let me be clear about this now. If you have kids living in your house, you might want to consider staging a secured defensive firearm in *their* room. Why? If those kids are asleep or if those kids are playing, you may instinctively move to that room to protect your kids.

If you end up in the kids' room and you don't have a firearm with you, your next step would either be to barricade without the benefit of a potent defensive tool or to move with your children to the location where you have staged your firearm. Obviously, neither choice is optimal, and the latter exposes you to a confrontation (with kids present) that you may have otherwise avoided. Too, your child's closet isn't where most people think of keeping a firearm.

Don't let your emotions override logic: If you have a firearm inside of a quick-access safe that is *secure*, you shouldn't have to worry about your kids having unauthorized access to it. If such a unit is locked, and if the safe is secured to the wall, your gun inside is ultimately no more accessible there than it is in the same safe kept in your room, or in a closet down the hallway, or in drawer. You shouldn't have to worry about your kids getting into your firearm when they're not supposed to, because you've educated them, they know the consequences, and they know how to act responsibly around firearms. And truly, if you can't trust your kids not to break into a firearms safe just because it's in their room, you may have more immediate problems than home security.

BUMPS IN THE NIGHT

Your bedroom is probably a place in which you spend a lot of time, especially at night, and so this place deserves a little extra attention regarding the issue of gun staging.

If you are awakened by an intruder, you want to have quick access to a firearm. There isn't a better "middle of the night," quick-access solution than a bedside holster. Holsters designed to attach directly to the side of your bed are made to hold a variety of different handguns. Bedside holsters make your defensive tool very easily accessible. Even when you are under the covers, you can reach down and establish a solid grip on the firearm, just as you would from any other holster worn on your body. Of course, a firearm in a bedside holster isn't really secure, so you will probably only want one there while you are actually in bed and, even then, only if you trust everyone else in the house to know to leave it alone (i.e., small, curious toddlers or preschoolers in the home would probably negate the use of such a holster).

Often, the bedroom is going to be your last barricade area. If you are there, there may be two, three, or four doors between yourself and the outside of your home. If you can get the family in your house behind you in this area, the bedroom is a great last position of defense.

At a last defensive position, you might want to have a very capable defensive long gun with which you can protect yourself. Usually, a defensive long gun (rifle or shotgun) will be staged with ammunition. Of course, if it's without ammunition, you're going to want to make sure that ammunition is close by and easily accessible. Storing a semi-automatic rifle unloaded and with a loaded magazine staged nearby is very common and a plausible solution, when you don't have a quick-access secure solution or can't otherwise stage a loaded gun.

Defensive long guns are often staged in an unloaded state, but with ammunition nearby, especially when they're staged in a last position of defense, such as a bedroom often becomes. If this is your choice for a staged weapon, make sure its ammunition source is close at hand and that you've practiced getting the gun loaded in a speedy manner.

One more note on long guns. If you are planning to use a lever-action rifle or a tube-fed shotgun, it's important to remember that these firearms are somewhat slow and complex to load. I would not consider either type of gun in an unloaded state to be an adequate worst-case scenario home-defense gun; tube-fed long guns should at least have their magazines loaded, even if you choose not to stage them with a round in the chamber. If, however, you are planning to use a double-barreled shotgun, these guns can be loaded very simply and quickly and, so, storing them unloaded does not disqualify them as a viable choice, provided ammunition is staged in a way to make loading as efficient as possible.

• • •

Ultimately where you keep your firearm is going to be up to you and your family. Making sure your guns are in the right place, the responsible place, to stage a firearm is one of the most important obligations you have as a firearms owner.

CHAPTER 7

CARRYING INSIDE YOUR HOME:

OPEN OR CONCEALED?

Not everyone wants, needs, or can stage a gun.
Carrying on your body is the answer, but how do you
go about that while you're "safe" in your home and
trying not to burn the kids' dinner?

The place you will always have a gun at the ready is on your body. While most people do not consider actually physically carrying a firearm while they are in their home, it may be the best choice. If you have a large home, if you have a crowded home, if you are in a high-risk environment, or if you do not own a method for securing a loaded firearm, carrying at home may be your best (and only) option.

Inside our homes, a lot of people think they might just carry *openly*, because they're not worried about offending anyone, it's legal, and they're going to be able to respond faster if someone comes into their home. The fact is that presentation from open carry may not be much faster than from concealment.

When I've conducted experiments comparing typical presentation times between open and concealed carry, I've found there is less than a third of a second in difference. Yes, you have to take into consideration that, naturally, anytime we measure presentation times, we are really measuring performance when we *know* we are going to be presenting. In the real world, of course, we're going to be responding to an attack we most likely are not expecting at all. We'll also be incorporating our body's natural reactions and many other considerations and distractions. None of these things will make our presentation faster—only slower. So, if we are looking at a two- to three-second presentation time to a first chest shot, at typical defensive distances

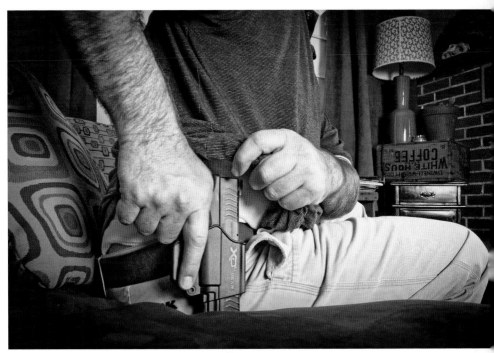

The truth is, presenting from concealment is only fractionally slower than presenting from an open carry position. That said, concealed carry has the element of surprise as a benefit, something carrying openly clearly does not.

and under realistic circumstances, an extra third of a second isn't really that much. Sure, our gut reaction is that every fraction of a second could be the difference between life and death, but let's factor in the negative aspects of carrying openly, before we start chasing tenths on a timer.

When someone bursts through your home's door and finds you with your family, one of the first things you're likely to do is try to get both the intruder and your family to calm down. You'll also try to get your family behind you, while you're saying to the intruder, "Sir, you're in the wrong place, stop, stay back, leave us alone … ." All the while, people are screaming and crying, and they'll be moving in a variety of directions. *Imagine it. This could happen to you.*

In such a situation, there are a lot of things going on. As I said before, these are chaotic situations. If you are carrying openly, now you have to add into all this chaos the imperative need to immediately deal with either using your gun or surrendering it.

Surrender your gun? If the bad guy sees your gun, you will likely have no good option. If he enters the home with a gun drawn and pointed at you and your family, trying to draw and shoot your gun before the intruder can hurt someone is a very sketchy proposition. At the same time, surrendering your gun could be suicidal.

Now, consider the same situation, but now you're in your home and carrying concealed. Now you have the tactical advantage in almost every variation of how this scenario can play out. Only if the intruder actually came in already shooting would you be compelled to draw immediately. Otherwise, you can wait to act for a moment when the intruder is distracted. Maybe you can negotiate or maneuver to get your family out of the line of his fire before you draw. Maybe you can even end the incident without gunplay. Either way, the advantages are significantly in your favor if you're carrying concealed in almost every case, and you certainly have more options.

It's important for you to understand that, in an actual event, you're not going to be sitting on the couch, relaxing with your family and watching a movie, and magically whip your gun out and stop a threat bursting through your front door. There's going to be a *reaction* moment. You're going to have a startled response. You're going to focus on the bad guy and simply be trying to figure out what is going on. You might look at your family. There are many things to factor in, before you make any decisions about actions you're going to take. In other words, this will not be about the raw presentation time you get when you're standing on a range practicing.

Before you decide whether to carry concealed or openly in your home, I need to emphasize again that, by concealing, you're not giving up very much at all, in terms of real time, when you decide to go for your gun, but you *are* gaining a *huge* amount in terms of that surprise—that response, that reaction, when you decide that the right opportunity is there for you to go for your firearm to protect you and your family inside your home.

CHAPTER 8

THE HOME ADVANTAGE:

DEFINING YOUR BEST DEFENSIVE POSITIONS

It's 10 p.m., the kids are in bed, and you're watching the late evening newscast, when you hear the sound of shattering glass coming from the kitchen. **Where do you go to defend you and your household?**

Two-story homes hold the advantage for you, when you can acquire the second floor and the threat is below. Height can provide you a way to observe a threat as you and your family retreat (evade) without necessarily being seen by that threat. Too, if you must engage a threat with a firearm from such a position, it's easier to shoot down than it is up.

In the moment of an imminent home invasion, you need to quickly assess where you are, where your family members might be, and where the threat is likely to enter your home. Whether you're near the entryway, in the middle of your house in a common area, or already in your bedroom, the decision of where to position yourself is one of the most important tactical considerations you can make.

When it comes to positioning yourself inside your home during an imminent home invasion, you're going to have a lot of options. This is where we start looking at the evasion and barricade steps in more detail. For the purposes of this discussion, we'll assume you are either carrying a gun or are able to arm yourself with one in the location we're discussing. Naturally, if you need to move into a specific location to arm yourself, that will dictate your position for armed home-defense. Remember that being armed doesn't always mean a gun, though a gun is certainly the most potent way to defend yourself.

If you spend a lot of time in your kitchen, thinking about how you'd respond to that imminent home invasion from that location is very important. So, let's say you're in your kitchen, the entryway's around the corner, and you experience a break-in. The first thing you might do is try to back away from that entryway, maybe get yourself behind some kind of concealment or cover (these are two different things). If you aren't alone in the home, such movement may be the best you can do, and that's fine for the moment, because you have evaded the immediate threat and barricaded yourself. That puts you in a position to respond, immediately if necessary, before the threat can reach your family. You can be there, tucked around a corner with your gun in the ready position, calling out to the family, maybe getting on a cell phone and making that call to the police. This may be your first defensible position and better than any other.

What about your den or living room? Of course, many people spend a fair amount of time sitting on the couch watching TV, playing games, reading, and talking with their families. From the couch, you have a couple options, as you respond to a break-in. For instance, if someone's trying to burst in through your front door or even just banging on the door enough to alarm you, your first instinct is going to be to investigate. You will naturally want to know what's going on at the door. But understand now, that

that is probably one of the *worst* things you could do. Rather than run towards the entryway where the bad guy's coming in, you should probably stay put or evade to an even better defensible position, remembering that, if there are other people in the home, their positions may dictate your movement or limit your options.

If you feel irresistibly compelled to investigate, think of how you can observe the doorway without moving towards it. Maybe you can look out a window and see who's banging on the door—maybe even from an *upstairs* window! Or, perhaps, you can position yourself so that you will see who comes through immediately, without actually being in *their* line of travel or field of view.

If your couch is directly in front of the door coming under assault, figure out the first place you can move to that will

If unauthorized access to your firearm isn't your top concern, perhaps because you live alone, then staging a gun in a pantry cabinet when you spend a lot of time in your kitchen can be a sound idea. It's not someplace a thief would look for a gun if you weren't home, and such a staging location can provide the benefit of the element of surprise, if you found yourself trapped or barricaded there.

put you off the angle of how the bad guy is traveling, but one that still puts you in a defensible position. An adjacent room off of the main living area, would be an example.

As you think about your home and the various entryways, you can plan defensive positions based on how much warning you have that a threat is present. If you have motion lights or perimeter or driveway alarms, you may have quite a bit of warning, relatively speaking. A home alarm system or a barking dog may also let you know that someone is entering your home, before you would otherwise know it. If you find yourself seeing or hearing a threat yourself, you probably have *less* time to act—and less time to act means less time to move and put yourself in a better position. If you do have time to move, a bedroom may be the place you decide to establish your most secure and defensible barricade.

The most likely movements of the bad guy through the floor plan of your home is a guiding issue. Put yourself in the shoes of the criminal. Think about how such an intruder is likely to move through you home. This will help you determine where you are both least likely to be found and best able to defend yourself. Balancing those two factors is how you determine the preferred barricade location. Remember, you know the terrain, so you've got the cover or at least the concealment. Think about how to use your home to *your* advantage. Are you looking at a reflection in a mirror or in a framed picture? It shouldn't be hard for you to imagine a threat's movement and possibly even predict where you can avoid or intercept them.

There's a knock at your front door, loud and hard and unexpected. If you really want to know what's out there, a smart move would be to get *away* from the sound, maybe to a second floor if possible, and observe the area from a safer position (and, if you can, one least observable from the outside), rather than through your door's side glass or even its peephole.

It's been shown that, typically, you will be somewhere between nine and 15 feet from a threat, when it comes time to engage them with a firearm. When establishing your various barricade positions, it's a good idea to pace off this range and work through, both mentally and with dry-fire (no ammo) drills, how you might have to defend yourself from these locations. Such exercises can help fine-tune your barricade positions and optimize your potential for a successful outcome.

9-15 feet

As mentioned earlier in the book, you want to maintain your distance from a threat, if possible. This means that, when you think about your barricade position, you want to make sure you will not be in immediate contact with your threat when a final confrontation is forced. This rules out closets, bathrooms, and other very small rooms, with one exception: if you are unarmed and either counting on hiding or relying on hand-to-hand skills if there is a confrontation. In that case, you are actually better served by being within arm's reach when you begin your defense.

If you are using a firearm to defend yourself, nine to 15 feet is the typical dis-

tance at which you'll be, when the threat rounds the last corner or breaks through the last door. This is the distance at which I've seen people of various physical and mental abilities perform consistently well across live fire, simulation, and force-on-force training environments. According to Tom Givens' data (the most extensive collection of data on personal-defense shootings that I am aware of), this is also the most common defensive shooting distance.

This distance range is optimum for both increasing your ability to respond effectively and decreasing the likelihood that the threat can touch you to harm

BARRICADE POSITION

Best position: 90 degrees offline from threat's direction of entry.

One of the most ideal positions you can take at your last, barricaded position, is one at a 90-degree angle from the point of entry at which the threat will be coming (the model here is clearly at a 90-degree angle from the bedroom door). In such a position, you will be out of both the immediate line of sight and line of travel of the threat, while the opposite is true for the threat.

Stairwells make excellent "choke points," places where you (the one with the firearm), can defend against an immediate threat while your family members coordinate to get to a designated barricade position behind you. Your advantage is amplified when you can hold a defensive position a level above your threat.

you and/or affect your ability to defend yourself. As an example, by setting yourself up in a corner of a bedroom that is at the optimum distance from the doorway and also 90 degrees offline from the line of travel as the door is breached, you are putting yourself in an excellent defensive position with a firearm.

Being 90 degrees off angle from the direction of the bad guy's movement means that after he breaks through the door, you'll be out of the direct line of fire if he has a gun and out of his direct view as he enters the room, so you'll have at least a fraction of a second advantage in your response. This extra time can also be applied to a last confirmation that you actually need to defend yourself. While it seems far-fetched, it is possible that you misunderstood what was going on. It could be a family member thinking they are coming to help you for some reason or a neighbor trying to get you to help with a medical emergency. You do *not* want to shoot unless you absolutely need to—make no assumptions.

Naturally, the presence of family members or others you care about inside your home may have a strong influence on your options for positioning yourself. Moving by yourself to your bedroom, locking the deadbolt, retrieving your firearm, and calling the police while you hear your family members fighting a threat outside the door in the hallway isn't really an option. If you have family spread out around the house at any given time, you should thing about "choke points" that you can defend, while they execute the broader home-defense plan and make their way to the preferred barricade location. Hallway corners and stairwells make the best choke points. In a two-level home, positioning yourself at the top of a stairwell, while your family situates itself in a safer location behind you and the bad guy is downstairs, is about as good as it can get if you are not all together behind a locked door. While you won't have the 90-degree offline advantage, you would be holding the high ground.

Being positioned above your attacker is a *huge* advantage, when defending yourself with a firearm. If your threat is armed with a contact weapon (knife, club, etc.), and they are foolish enough to advance up the steps towards you, you really can't ask for a better scenario. If your threat has a firearm and presses their attack, it is generally harder to shoot in an upward direction than it is in a downward, both because of human anatomy and balance, as well as natural fighting postures.

If your home is on a single level or if the stairway is not available to you, the corner of a hallway can also make a great defensive position. By placing yourself at a hall corner when you know the intruder is beyond the other end and likely coming to it, you can take maximum advantage of knowing where the threat will appear. This is similar to being barricaded in a room. Should the intruder present himself and need to be addressed, you can be much more prepared than if you are moving around your house and unsure of where the threat is or may emerge from. Too, with your family behind you hiding or behind a barricade, the corner of a hall can provide some amount of protection for you as you hide much of your body behind the corner and away from the threat's direction of approach.

CHAPTER 9

DRESS REHEARSAL:

HOME INVASION RESPONSE DRILLS

Home invasions come equipped with lots of unanswered questions—What's he gonna do? Where's he gonna go? What's he gonna take? Who's he gonna hurt? **Your live-action practice routine will help you deal with the answers to those questions.**

'm sure you remember fire drills from your time at elementary school. As an adult, now, you probably know you're supposed to have a plan for you and your family to follow in case your home catches fire. Maybe you've even run a fire drill at your house. (Of course, if you don't have a fire plan and haven't practiced it, you *should*!) But just thinking about such plans and talking about it with your family isn't enough. You need to actually *act out* what it is you're all supposed to do. That may mean running out the back door or escaping through an alternate route. Your family may all meet up at the big tree in a neighbor's yard or down the street at the corner. After you have walked through the drills and some alternatives, you should run through it at full speed. You may even decide to wake everyone up one evening and run them through the fire plan when they aren't expecting it.

I can't think of anyone who can't see the sense and reasonableness of such a plan. So, in that same vein, and because you're already invested in this book and its topic, it should also make sense and be reasonable to you to have a home-defense plan and run drills with it!

In 2009, a friend of mine went out for a massage. His home was invaded by armed attackers shortly after he left. His wife and children were inside—and they had no plan for home-defense.

It didn't have to be that way. My friend is a very successful personal-defense instructor. Yet his family had no home-defense plan and, so, of course, hadn't rehearsed any response actions to an intrusion event. Luckily, his son was alone upstairs and saw the gunman push through the door and chase his mom through the house towards the room his younger sisters were in. The son acted quickly and resisted the instinctive urge to run and protect his family and instead called the police, who arrived very shortly thereafter. (The police scared away the attackers, who ran from the home, and they were later caught and arrested.)

In this case, the proximity of the police and some good fortune all transpired to avoid a tragedy. In the wake of that incident, my friend created a home-defense plan, reinforced the security of his home, obtained a handgun and a quick-access safe, purchased a guard dog, and took several other steps to prepare for any future incident of the same sort.

By reading this book and thinking about your plan ahead of time, you are several steps ahead of my friend's very lucky family. But, just reading this book or simply thinking about what you would do simply isn't enough. Talking to your family (or roommates) about what you would do also isn't enough. Only when you have actually run through the motions, possibly many times, should you hope to be able to execute your plan and capitalize on everything you're learning here. Even if you live alone, running through your drills and putting the fundamentals of home-defense into play from time to time is vital to your ability to perform as you would like to in an actual emergency.

What kind of plan do you have in place if you're all sitting in the living room and watching a movie, when someone smashes through a sliding glass

From the "mailman" who doesn't look quite right, to the guy sneaking in through your unlocked back door while you're relaxing in the living room, there are a slew of predators out there looking to make their living off of easy targets. Having a plan for that fake delivery guy getting through that chain or having a pistol located near your couch can help you survive the encounters like these you hope never happen, but just might.

door? What if you and your family are sitting at the dining room table eating dinner, and all of a sudden someone bursts in through the front door? What if someone bursts in through the rear door?

Maybe you get a little bit of warning. You hear a car screech to a halt in front of your home. You hear loud sounds outside, and you hear yelling. Maybe you hear someone banging on your door. Maybe you have a reinforced door, and that's what's keeping them outside for the first 15 to 30 seconds of a violent home invasion. *What exactly are you going to do?*

First thing you need to think about, as we discussed in the last chapter, is where you're going to go. At the same time, acknowledge what your *natural* reaction is going to be, if you hear a loud banging at your front door? It's probably going to be to look towards your front door, and you're probably going to want to move towards it.

This is the time to enact your plan and use your fundamental home-defense tactics—still, I know, and you *should* know, that acting on that plan instead of investigating the thump at the door, is *not* likely to happen *if you haven't practiced*. And, of course, the sound of breaking glass at the rear of your house while you're in the living room certainly is not going to be the appropriate time to devise a plan on the fly and then try to share that plan with your family.

Lots of you will question that last sentence. You're smart, conscious of things around you, and secure in your home, and you may (maybe even probably) figure your instincts will get you through the crisis of an invasion. But, during a crisis, emotions will be running high and your instincts will be working overtime—and it's just those things that will inhibit the decisions that will correctly enact a complex series of steps. What happens, instead, is that people often improvise or default to natural reactions. That can mean running towards the door (and the threat) to investigate or even just freezing in place and not taking any action at all. Having a plan in place, discussing it ahead of time, and running drills with it means you'll be much more apt to actually *put that into action when the time comes.*

Repeated exposure to anything is what leads to *recognition*. Recognition is the method of the expert, and you want to be become a home-defense expert. Only through repeated exposure, that exposure spread out over time, will you and your family be able to count on executing your home-defense plans like experts. And just like any coordinated team, you need to learn to act together during practices before the "big game."

What else will you think about, when it comes to your immediate plan? Not just where will you go or where will you look, but what will you *do*? If someone is trying to invade your home, probably one of the most important things you can do right away is make a phone call. In your plan, who's responsibility is it to get to that phone? Which phone will they use? Maybe you still have a landline in your house that you (obviously) know is kept in one place. It's always going to be there. If you can get to that phone, you can make the call you need to make. What if your home doesn't have a land line anymore? Do you always keep your cell phone in the same place, when it's in the house? Do you always charge it in the same place?

Did you know that an old cell phone, one that's not on a contract anymore nor doesn't have a service plan, can still make emergency 9-1-1 calls? If you keep an old cell phone on a charger in your barricade area or in your staging area, you can know there is always going to be a phone for you (or someone else) to use to call the police. Wherever it is that you're going to barricade, you can get to that phone and make an emergency call,

because it's on the charger and ready to go. This is one of the simplest things a modern family can do to better prepare for a worst-case scenario.

If you asked them right now, does your family know that, if there's an emergency, if there's some kind of imminent danger, they're supposed to go in a specific place, they're supposed to do specific things? Does your plan include other family members accessing firearms? Where are those guns? Do they have a plan to be able to get to them? Are they thinking ahead of time

about where they're going to be? Do you have firearms staged around you home in various places? *If so, how do you keep multiple family members all from being armed, scared, and moving through the house separately but at the same time— what steps have you taken to avoid tragic accidents in the heat of the moment?*

I suggest you come up with a family security word you can you use only during these types of emergencies that lets others in your household know that someone they do not need to be afraid of is coming around a corner or through a door. Make the word something that is absolutely not going to get used or that could be confusing during a dynamic critical incident ("antelope," "bubble gum" "spaghetti," something along those lines would be good options). Once you establish the family safety word, keep it secure. If you do find out that anyone has revealed it to an outsider, change it!

Does every family member know how to use all the firearms you have in the house, or are there some members of the family who can use only certain guns? Are you the only one who's going to be able to get to the firearm during an incident? If so, do your family members have other responsibilities, such as making phone calls, holding a light source, locking doors, creating barricades, and setting alarms?

Regardless your plan, it is vital you talk to your family and actually rehearse the plan. You should also rehearse your plan a couple different ways. The front door bursts open, what do you do? There's a banging at the house's rear sliding glass door, what do you do? There's a screeching of tires in front of your house and some guys yelling, maybe even shots fired, a situation that doesn't involve you, what then? Make sure your family understands the concept of pre-cursor cues and how to utilize them to execute their plan without hesitation.

Last, make sure that one of the variables you work into your plan is the possibility of missing family members. Who takes over for whom when someone is missing? What if *you* are missing? Answer these questions and others, and you'll not only have Plan A, but Plans B through Z, as well.

DID YOU KNOW THAT AN OLD CELL PHONE, ONE THAT'S NOT ON A CONTRACT ANYMORE, CAN STILL MAKE EMERGENCY 9-1-1 CALLS? KEEP THAT PHONE ON A CHARGER IN YOUR SAFE AREA, AND YOU'LL ALWAYS HAVE A WAY TO CONTACT HELP.

CHAPTER 10

SHOOTING INDOORS: WHERE DOES YOUR BULLET STOP?

Before you're faced with having to do away with some uninvited guy in a ski mask bent on doing you in, you must think about where your bullet's going and what it's going to hit if you miss.

What would you see if you were barricaded in your bedroom, on the phone with the police, family behind you, firearm in hand, hoping that no one was going to come through the door? Whatever you are looking at is the most likely "backstop" for defensive gunfire in your home. If that intruder did come through the door and was identified as a lethal threat, this is the exact angle at which you would most likely engage them with your firearm.

But, what if you weren't able to get the family behind you before that moment? Or what if that which you're looking at is the inside of your home's exterior wall or a shared wall with another residence. If that was the case and if you were to shoot at a person at that angle and have a miss, or should your bullet push through the intruder, you would need a safe backstop there.

IT'S ALL IN THE BOOKS (MOSTLY)

The good news is that having a solid backstop for your bullets to land doesn't necessarily mean armor plating. My favorite recommendation for a safe backstop in your home is books. Not only can books stop bullets, having books in your house encourages reading, learning, and increased knowledge. Seriously, that, to me, is a huge win-win. You can arrange the books to cover almost every square inch of surface area at the likely angles you'd be shooting during an intrusion, and so have a very high chance of stopping any rounds that might miss your threat.

Interior home walls generally do *not* do a good job of stopping bullets or shotgun pellets. Only the lightest shotgun loads will be stopped by typical drywall, and I wouldn't recommend such ammunition as a primary choice for home-defense; you are much better off thinking

Stacks and shelves of books are an excellent backstop for bullets or shot that have missed their intended mark or those that might have passed through an intruder.

about where your bullets could go and practicing to be confident in hitting your target with practical and adequately powerful ammunition, than you are choosing an anemic load for your defensive firearm for fear of over-penetration. Choose appropriately powerful rounds, then remember to tie in the thinking about the background you might be shooting into as just part of being a responsible defensive firearms owner.

During extensive and repeated testing, I have found that almost no common household item or piece of furniture will reliably stop bullets except for books. Not TVs, not refrigerators, and not couches, desks, mattresses, or doors. The concept of safe backstops being made out of bookshelves can be applied to various areas in your home, not just a living room or den, indeed, any area you think represents the likely background on which a defensive shot could land. You can also set up bookshelves as "safe havens" or additional barricade positions

in the case you or a family member cannot get to you primary planned location.

BALLISTIC ARMOR

While thinking about the places where your own bullets might land, you should also naturally consider protecting your family from an intruder's shots. Although seen as extreme by many, one way is to purchase ballistic armor vests.

Vests are available from a variety of companies and are completely legal in most places. In fact, several years ago, a company called U.S. Palm began offering high-quality ballistic armor at affordable prices specifically to those interested in family home-defense. I have one of their vests, along with others from my days of working in law enforcement and executive protection. Keep in mind, however, that vests only protect the parts of the body they cover—thus, a kid hiding behind a properly prepared bookshelf is completely protected from just about any type of typical defensive firearm round.

Having bullet-resistant armor may seem extreme, but, if your budget allows and more fundamental defensive steps have also been taken, staging a vest for yourself and/or family members may not be an outrageous idea.

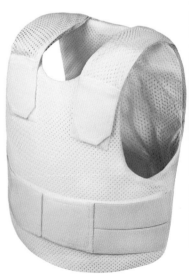

CHAPTER 11

ARMED AND ON THE MOVE

You're almost always better off shooting while you're standing still and in a static location. **Sometimes, that's just not an option.**

At home and on the range, practice moving as a team to identify and eliminate threats.

One of the great frustrations I have in my social life is having to endure stories from friends or acquaintances about that one time when they heard something at night, got their gun, and went to investigate. Generally, the response they expect from me is a something much closer to a high-five than a slap upside the head, but they usually get the latter, at least verbally. Depending on the setting and how good a friend they are, the response they get can varies from an "Oh," as I try to change the subject, right up to a blunt "You're lucky you didn't get killed or have to kill someone, because that's exactly what I recommend people *not* do."

The No. 1 rule of personal-defense is to avoid confrontation. If you leave a safe position and move to a position that could be less safe, you are pretty clearly violating that rule. Moving into an unknown area exposes you to more danger than staying put most of the time, especially if you really don't know what you're going to be dealing with. When you are still, you can put your back to a wall or corner and prevent yourself from being ambushed from behind, but, if you start moving, you inevitably open yourself up to attack from at least two directions.

With that in mind, you certainly wouldn't want to believe that you can safely move through your house alone, covering every possible angle of attack. Even military special operations personnel and S.W.A.T. team members train to move through buildings as a team and require at least two people to enter every room or go around every corner. I've had the honor of running training

in this area for U.S. Navy S.E.A.L.s and U.S. Army Green Berets, and even these highly trained warriors move at least in pairs when performing their versions of these maneuvers.

Now, cap off what I know about such movement with the fact that nearly every one of those "investigation" stories I'm told about ends with it having been nothing at all or someone who wasn't actually a threat having made the noise. Why put yourself in the position of moving around with a gun in your hand, potentially pointing it at a family member or friend? Moving through your home while armed is something you should do only if you truly need to.

As I always say to my students, "I don't wear a badge anymore, and I don't have flashy red or blue lights on my car. I don't *need* to go towards the bad guy." The entire reason for having a plan for armed home-defense is so that you can *follow it*. The plan, as we've discussed, is to evade and barricade, while you call the police and let them respond to deal with the threat. If it doesn't work out that way, you still want to use your plan to stack the odds in your favor. If you must fight, you are much better off fighting from your barricaded position and ambushing the threat as he enters, than you are moving through your house and possibly getting ambushed yourself.

Why might you need to move through your home while armed and you have an intruder in your midst? As we've already covered, you may be moving to your barricade point where you expect your family to be waiting. If you've rehearsed a plan, you should try to stick to it whenever possible. However, if you believe your family is at the barricade point and the intruder is heading towards them, you would likely be compelled to move towards them while armed. Likewise, if you hear a family member calling for help, you would naturally be compelled to move. Honestly, as a parent, I don't believe anyone would *not* move through their home to help their children, regardless the risk. Too, absent a panicked cry, you may also have solid reason to believe there's a threat of danger to a family member, especially if one or more of your family members are unaccounted for. In this case, you would also be understandably compelled to move. Yet another plausible scenario would be if you and your family are together, but in an exposed area that is not easily defendable. In this case, you might be better served by moving to a barricade point.

Moving through your home with an intruder present is risky business. It exposes you to ambush, and you may encounter your threat up close and personal sooner than you anticipated. In all, it's best not to move other than to your barricaded position, but, if you must move, do everything you can not to be seen by the threat, while also minimizing your overall physical exposure to ambush and attack.

Whenever you are moving through your home with an intruder in it (armed or not), your No. 1 priority must be to avoid being ambushed by someone who sees you coming. Your secondary concern should be to try to see the threat before they see you. Ultimately, you need to be prepared for a meeting at the same time or for them to see you first—either would be considered an ambush.

If you are armed, you must be very careful not to make a tragic mistake. Given that many of the things that happen in the home and startle you turn out to be false alarms or are simply misunderstandings, you must factor in some response time before your use of a firearm. If you were to walk through the home with your finger on the trigger and holding the gun out at extension in front of you, you would be creating several potential tactical failure points that could

lead to tragedy, for instance, if you had a neighbor's child in the house playing a prank or looking for help, instead of a lethal threat you imagined some unexpected noise to be. Similarly, there have been many cases (usually involving alcohol), that have mistakenly lead to people being shot after they broke into a home or apartment they believed was theirs.

When I am running home-defense tactics courses, using role players and force-on-force training equipment, one of our final scenarios is a home break-in by someone in a confused state that explicitly does *nothing* threatening to any member of the household. Unfortunately, human nature often gets the better of our students, and they will rush towards the sounds of the person ranting in their living room instead of staying put and calling the police. And even though they never had a reason to shoot, the vast majority would find themselves in a discussion with the role player, with their gun out and pointed at them.

In these types of scenarios, our role players are trained to follow strict scripts and specifically told to avoid giving any perception that they posed an overt threat to anyone in the home. They would mutter, stumble, possibly break something, but they would never come towards the homeowner or any family member, nor even make any verbal threats. Without these controls, I have no doubt that the actions of many students would result in a confrontation with a real person, particularly one deranged, disturbed, or drunk enough to be confused about where they live.

Sadly, this exact scenario played out a handful of years ago, in Colorado,

when a homeowner shot a drunk college student who was trying to enter the wrong house. The real tragedy of this incident is that the homeowner could've been barricaded in the home and on the phone with the police, as there was plenty of warning that the young man was trying to gain entry. Instead, the homeowner positioned himself with a gun in hand, inside the room the student was entering into (and exposed to a threat, if the intruder had, in fact, been armed with a gun), and watched the man break through a pane of glass to open the door. What is worse is that the homeowner had moved through the house, with his gun, to get to the point of entry. As the intruder entered, the man shot him. There was no objective evidence of evil intent, but the homeowner perceived there was. Now, in many locales, a shooting like that is legal—but that doesn't mean it was necessary.

In my mind, if that homeowner had been around two more corners or behind two more doors and barricaded in a bedroom, there is a significant

If you anticipate having to move through your home, a paddle-type holster can instantly give you a safely holstered, quickly accessible gun, without the hassle of stringing on a belt beforehand.

Once the firearm is in hand (here and right), keep it close to your body, but ensure your finger is well away from the trigger as you move through the home.

chance no one would have been shot. As someone thinking about armed home-defense, you should remember that even if you use force and win, you have to live with the aftermath of that fight for the rest of your life. That aftermath might include legal, financial, social and emotional trauma.

If you do need to move through your home for a legitimately compelling reason, follow the tips by Craig Douglas that can be found at the end of this chapter. If possible, you should use a family member to "watch your back" as you move, covering areas with their eyes that you can't see as you look forward.

Keep in mind, too, that, when it comes to moving with a gun, it is always going to be easier for you to control a handgun held in the High Compressed Ready position than it is to control a long gun, should you be attacked by a threat within two arms' reach (more on this in Chapters 20 and 22). For instance, if you need to sling your rifle or shotgun to carry a child, make a phone call, or secure a door, getting that long gun back into your hands to deal with a lethal threat close to you can be very awkward. For these reasons, I generally advise those not trained in handling a long gun in specifically in close quarters to rely on their handgun.

In fact, for those with very little training who choose to move with firearms through buildings, but who *are* familiar with presentation of a firearm from a holster, I often recommend they consider wearing the holstered firearm in the house, but not to put the gun in

their hand until they have confirmed there is actually a threat in the home. While this may sound odd to those familiar with "tactical training," the reality is that most people without any formal experience in this area are going to be much better off knowing their gun is secure until they *know* they need it, than they are with the gun out and potentially pointing at family members or within grabbing reach of a threat.

By putting on a paddle holster when you retrieve your gun from its staging area, leaving a gun you are already carrying in its holster, or simply putting on a belt and holster combination (or "battle belt") when you enact your home-defense plan, you ensure that you have a gun (and possibly a light, magazines, medical equipment, doorstops, etc.), and you keep yourself at least two steps from a tragic mistake (drawing and firing when you are startled). In the event you *do* have an active violent intruder, you can still quickly get the gun into the ready or shooting position, just as you have trained to do.

If you do need to carry your gun through your home in the ready position, the most important considerations are keeping your finger clearly away from the trigger and keeping the gun close to you. The details of techniques such as "slicing the pie" and "covering danger areas" that are taught to tactical teams are beyond the scope of this book and beyond the level of training in which most homeowners will ever have the opportunity to participate. Let those both be further reminders that moving through your home while armed when you think there might be an intruder inside is something to be avoided whenever possible.

10 TIPS FOR ARMED MOVEMENT IN STRUCTURES

▶ **TIP NO. 1:** There is no truly safe way to move through a home when there is a threat inside the home with you. Optimally, you will remain in place and let the intruder do the moving. If you do have to move for a specific reason, the best you can hope to do is manage the risks.

▶ **TIP NO. 2:** A structure is a 360-degree environment. Threats can come from any direction. Don't limit yourself to thinking your threat is around the corner you're at which you're looking or even on the same floor level as you. Your threat could be down the hall, behind you, at your feet hiding behind a couch, or up above you on a landing.

▶ **TIP NO. 3:** Learn to view your environment in terms of what you can't see. If you can see a threat, it is relatively easy to deal with. If you can't see it, that threat can be a bigger problem. Learn to look at edges, not holes. The opening of a door isn't as important a place to focus as the two side edges, from which a threat could emerge. Arguably, you could also be attacked from the top edge. This is important to remember as you move. Check many danger areas at once.

▶ **TIP NO. 4:** There are three potential planes of visual impediment—vertical, horizontal, diagonal. Vertical planes are corners and doorways. Horizontal planes are generally furniture and countertops or islands. Diagonal planes will almost always be stairways, in a home-defense scenario. Always seek distance from a plane of visual impediment. You want to be as far away from these planes as you possibly can be to maximize your field of view beyond them.

▶ **TIP NO. 5:** Your "shooting platform" must conform to the plane of visual impediment. In order to maximize your safety through minimizing your exposure around corners, your stance must adapt so that you don't telegraph elbows, knees, and feet around corners before your eyes can see a threat. This also means you should train for shooting in a variety of unorthodox shooting positions, when you are at the range.

By Craig Douglas

Craig Douglas, of the personal protection company Shivwerks, is one of the leading trainers in the industry and has a great deal of experience teaching on the topic of moving while armed. His tips will help you understand the myriad problems to which you open up yourself if you choose to move while armed, as well as guide you in performing as well as possible if you must move.

▶ TIP NO. 6: Pace your movements appropriately, to solve the problems or deal with exigent circumstances.
Take as much time as possible to work angles and enter new danger areas. You want to see as much as you can before you commit to moving around a corner or exposing yourself to a new danger area. Of course, if the reason for your movement is the need to rescue a screaming child, you will need to pick up your pace.

▶ TIP NO. 7: WHEN YOU ARE MOVING ALONE, YOU ARE ALWAYS EXPOSED IN AT LEAST TWO DIRECTIONS.
Unlike being in a fixed position with your "back against the wall," when you are moving, you must be open to attack from at least two directions. You cannot assume that your threat is definitely in front of your direction of travel.

▶ TIP NO. 8: MAKE EVERY POSSIBLE ATTEMPT TO MINIMIZE MULTIPLE EXPOSURES.
If you can, adjust your route through a structure to lower the number of doorways and corners you can see (and be seen from!) at any given moment.

When you are forced to be exposed in many directions, minimize the time of exposure by changing your pace. You can mitigate the deficiencies of moving alone to some extent by moving faster to specific points of relatively increased safety. Your positioning between fast movements must be planned and precise, as you move through a structure.

▶ TIP NO. 9: MINIMIZE THE ANGLE OF POTENTIAL THREAT TO 45 DEGREES WHENEVER POSSIBLE.
If you can put your most significant danger areas within a 45-degree cone, it is more plausible that you will pick up movement from a threat in time to respond before an attack. The wider your potential area of responsibility, the less likely you are to be looking in the right place at the right time.

▶ TIP NO. 10: IF AN INTRUDER IS ENCOUNTERED, BE PREPARED FOR ANYTHING THEY MIGHT DO.
They may attack, they may flee, they may engage in dialogue. These kinds of problems are very mercurial, and the human factor must be accounted for— this is not a video game.

CHAPTER 12

AFTER YOU DIAL 9-1-1:

COMMUNICATING WITH LAW ENFORCEMENT

You will not have a trained law enforcement individual in your living room when you want one. Help them get there—and keep both of you safe— in the moments when you need them most.

Dialing 9-1-1 should be a top priority in the event of a home invasion. Before you press those numbers, know exactly what you need to convey to the dispatcher, so that help arrives as quickly as possible and so that, when it does arrive, both you and the police remain safe and in one piece.

Inevitably, if you have a problem inside of your home, if you need to use lethal force, if you need to use any force at all to defend yourself or your family, or if force is used against you, you're going to interact with law enforcement. Even if you just have to make the emergency phone call and it turns out to be a false alarm or the threat leaves without direct confrontation, the police will respond. You need to have a plan for dealing with law enforcement every bit as much as you do the bad guys.

Let's say you have someone trying to get into your house or someone has gotten in and you've been able to get into a barricade situation, you've been able to get our family behind us, and you've been able to get our firearm. Now you're on the phone about to make the emergency contact. As mentioned earlier in the book, when you call the emergency contact number, you need to be able to tell them five things.

- Where you are (address for dispatching of police)
- What's going on
- That you are armed (if true)
- Attacker description (if possible)
- Your description

Let's look at each of these things in greater detail.

The first thing you need to communicate to an emergency operator is exactly where you are, specifically, the address where the problem is occurring. While they may be able to track that information, you may be on a cellphone, you may be making the call from outside your home, you may be on a landline. There are a lot of variables here, and you can't be sure that things like apartment numbers and specific addresses are going to come up accurately. When I say that you need to tell them *exactly* where you are, I mean that you need to tell them everything they need to know to get help on the way to you and not the house next door, or the next neighborhood over, or Elm Street instead of where you live on Elm Drive. If your call is cut off after this point, at least the police will be sent to the right spot (and probably with some urgency, based on the likely tone of your voice and the fact that the call was cut off.)

Don't tell the operator you're in your bedroom, when they first ask where you are. Tell them the *address* first, then move

Staying calm and relaying the right information to a 9-1-1 dispatcher may be the toughest thing you ever have to do, but you must do exactly that. There are lots of people between you and help, and your clear, detailed information about what's going on in your emergency can mean the difference between life and death for everyone involved.

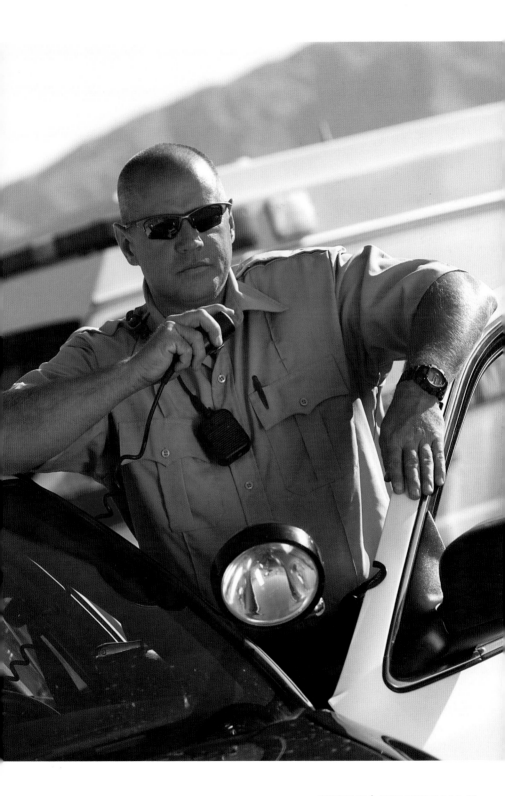

Once you are able to make contact with police, there will be lots of them at your doorstep. Make sure you've clearly identified to them who you are, what you and your family look like, where in the home you are, what the intruder looks like, whether you are armed, and any other pertinent information that will keep you or them from being accidentally shot.

on to the other items that are urgent to communicate. If you have time later in the call, you can describe the specific location ("Upstairs, last door on the right.")

The next thing you want to tell the emergency operator is what's going on. "A man's trying to get into my house, the man's got a knife"—whatever it is. Express as specifically as you can that you have an emergency and that you need help to be dispatched right away. The nature of the emergency is what

will dictate *their* urgency. If you calmly say that a stranger is in your backyard, you can expect a slow response. If you say that someone is shooting into your home, expect to see lights and hear sirens as quickly as possible given your location and the density of local law enforcement coverage. Police officers will be dispatched from non-urgent activities (traffic stops, investigations, etc.), to respond to someone who truly needs help. While you cannot count on the police to protect you (if you could, this book would not be necessary!), I do believe you absolutely can count on them to try if they know what is going on.

The next thing I advise you to tell the emergency operator is that you are armed. You want to make sure that the police officers responding to the scene know the good guy has a firearm. This way they don't think just anyone with a gun on the scene is automatically a bad guy. *This is not a political issue!* Police officers have a sometimes very dangerous job, and you are calling them into an threatening, emergency situation. This call is *their* dynamic critical incident, too, and they are being told that someone is in danger from a threat. They will be keyed up and looking for the people who pose a threat—any armed person they see could be the bad guy. Indeed, that's a reasonable first assumption. So telling them that you are armed sets the stage for them to prevent accidentally ending up in a tragic confrontation with you.

The next thing you want to be able to do, if you can, is describe the bad guy. Again, this let's you set the stage for the police officers to make the right decisions when they arrive. If the bad guy is recognized by the police when they show up, the officers and you will be safer, faster.

Last, you want to describe yourself and your family members to the emergency operator, for all of what should now be the obvious reasons. If the officer knows (because the dispatcher has told him), that the potential victim is armed, is also the home owner, and what you have on, the police officers are much more likely to give you that extra second, give the benefit

of the doubt, when they see you, and not immediately think that you are the bad guy and thereby unnecessarily escalate an already tense event.

When those police officers shows up, you're going to have direct interaction them. Let's take a look at how that should play out, in a perfect situation, when the police officer arrives at your home and you're armed.

Police Officer to Dispatcher: The rest of the house is clear. Is the homeowner still in the upstairs bedroom?

Dispatcher: Yes, they are on the line.

Dispatcher to You: The officer says that the house is clear and that you can come out.

You to Dispatcher: Yes, I believe the police officer's in the hallway. Can you have the officer call out for Susie? I want to make sure it's not the bad guy.

Dispatcher will relay message to officer.

Police Officer to you: Susie, you in there?

You to Dispatcher: All right, I heard him. I'm going to put the phone down.

You to Officer: Yes, sir.

Police Officer: Open the door for me, and let me see your hands. (Keep in mind that this is a completely reasonable request. As sick as it seems, people have faked 9-1-1 calls in order to ambush police officers before. It is also remotely possible that you have been taken hostage by the bad guy before the officer arrived, and that you are being ordered by your hostage taker to say everything is fine. Either way, the officers will need to verify that you are safe while still protecting themselves.)

At this point, you should holster or lay down your firearm. If you lay it down, be sure that it is not within reach of you or any family member.

You: Yes, sir. (Open the door, your hands showing through the opening first.) I do not have a firearm. The firearm is not in my hands, sir.

Police Officer: Okay, where's the firearm now?

You: Sir, right there, by the television.

Police Officer: Okay. Down on the ground, put your hands out.

You: Yes, sir. Yes, sir.

You should now follow the police officer's directions, and there's no need to be insulted or concerned about following them. Remember, you called them to come to your house, and now you need to finish the process of letting them make sure that everyone is safe and the scene is secure.

Let's go back in this scenario a bit. As you can imagine, when you think the police are about to come to your rescue, first and foremost you want to make sure that the person you're coming out of your barricade for *is* actually a police officer. The way you're going to do that is going to have to either be by trusting your gut about what you hear on the other side of the door or, preferably, setting up some type of a challenge or a code word with the dispatcher on the other end of the phone line. Think right now of what you want them to say. Obviously, if you have a family member named "Susie," then the example above would be a bad one.

Now let's say you're in an environment where you'd be worried that the bad guy can hear your code phrase because of thin walls or close spaces. You may need to come up with another way to verify that an officer is on the other side of the door, perhaps ask the dispatcher to have the officer tell them what color the carpet is or to describe a picture hanging on the wall near your door. At the point you finally believe there is a police officer on the other side, you're going to put the phone down, but don't disconnect the line. In fact, be sure that you don't hang up the phone at all once you have called 9-1-1 and until the situation is resolved.

•••

In summary, when you are going to make contact with the officer, you need to make sure he doesn't perceive you as a threat. Once you have survived the intruder's threat, your job then is to make sure you don't hurt or get hurt by responding law enforcement. You also need, at some point, to be ready to comply with the officers' instructions. Make sure they see your hands, make sure they know where your firearm is. Make sure you don't inadvertently put yourself in a position where you can get hurt and, of course, don't put yourself in a position where you feel compelled to defend yourself against a police officer who's just doing his job.

Interaction with law enforcement is an important part of home-defense. You might want to role-play this interaction with another family member, as part of your home-defense drills.

CHAPTER 13

SHOULD VERSUS COULD:

WHEN TO USE DEFENSIVE FORCE

Just because you can—and even if just
because you have a legal right to—doesn't
mean pulling the trigger's the best thing to do.

"When can I use lethal force to defend myself?"

That's a question I get a lot from students, as well as from a variety of people who contact me through the Internet. Whether it's on a forum, through social media, in person, or through the reading of one of my books (just like this one!), that question comes up often; it's clear to me that people wonder what the law says about whether or not they *can* use a firearm to defend themselves or their families.

While that certainly *is* an important question, it is not the *most* important question, with regards to the use of lethal force. Certainly, six months ahead of time, six days ahead of time, even six *minutes* ahead of time, you absolutely need to know what the laws are in your jurisdiction. You need to know what the laws are about owning firearms, you need to know what the laws are about having firearms inside your home for home-defense and, of course, for carrying firearms in public for the defense of yourself and your family. Yes, you need to follow those laws.

Okay, but what about during the event itself, in the actual moment of a home invasion, in the moment of an ambush, when you're faced with a lethal threat and you have the means to defend yourself and your family inside of your home? The question isn't *can* you use lethal force, it's always going to be *should* you use lethal force.

If you're in a situation where you have someone coming into your home with a lethal weapon—an axe, a club, a gun, a knife—it's an obvious point of judgment on your part that such a person means to hurt you or your family, plus you can see they have the opportunity to do so.

You absolutely *should* defend yourself and your family inside of that home. No, I am absolutely not advising you to break the law, but I am telling you that, if you believe that you or your family are in lethal jeopardy and there is no way to escape that jeopardy without potentially putting yourself at more risk, you should mount a defense under all legal systems that I am aware of. There is no guarantee that, in the aftermath, you will be judged to have acted appropriately, regardless of what the laws are, but you have to protect yourself. It is not just your right—I believe it is your *responsibility*.

Let's say you have someone who's pounding on your door with that same axe, and you have your family together are gathered in the living room. You can make your way to an alternative exit, look outside and see that the coast is clear, run out, probably with your cellphone in hand and calling the police, and escape. *If this is an option*, you absolutely should run out that back door and stay away. This is a somewhat controversial opinion, but it is one I believe in. Bravado and theatrics do not trump your safety.

Let me give you a specific example. If I'm sitting on the couch and I hear someone for five minutes trying to break my door down, I pull my firearm out, I sit in the ready position, get on the phone with the sheriff's office and say, "Hey, there's someone trying to break into my home, I'm afraid they're going to try to kill me, I have a firearm, and I will use it to defend myself and my family if I need to." Four minutes later, the guy bursts through the door, comes around the corner, I drop the phone, extend my handgun out, and shoot him. Now, that is probably going to be considered legal and acceptable in most of the United States. However, if I *could* have left my area in the house, gone behind a solidly barricaded door and several corners by moving upstairs to my bedroom, gotten on the phone, and made that same call, I think that should be the smarter choice.

I'm absolutely not advocating for a restriction of our rights to defend ourselves, nor am I saying we should change the laws to say you must try to escape or you must try to get away if you can. What I am saying is that *you absolutely should try to avoid shooting another human being if you can*. If you can avoid using a firearm to hurt someone else, if you can avoid needing to put yourself and your family and your neighborhood and your community through that trauma, if you can avoid the risk of prosecution, if you can avoid the risk of civil suit and all the things that go with that, you absolutely should.

The questions (and answers) of whether you can use a firearm for self-defense are ones you should research. The question of what you do at the exact moment you have the opportunity to protect your family with a firearm is a much different question.

Understanding the difference between should and could is an important part of being a responsibly armed firearms owner. At your home, the laws may be very different than they are at your workplace. At the places you live and work, the laws may be very different than they are at another family member's home when you're visiting, or in a hotel room when you're traveling in another state.

Understanding whether you can have the firearm available to you is a big *legal* issue. Understanding what to do at the

moment you absolutely need to defend yourself is much more *personal* and much more specific to your situation.

I'm not going to second-guess someone who says they needed to defend themselves and used a firearm to do so. But, if you stood just inside the entryway of your home, waiting for someone who could obviously hurt you and your family to burst through the doors just so that you *could* use your firearm, when your alternative could have been going to another room, barricading behind another door or two, and getting on the phone with the police, I'll say that you should have chosen the latter option. It's what I think your responsibility is and, ultimately, if you're in that situation and you are forced to defend yourself or your family, it's going to be much more obvious to anyone who investigates the situation that you did everything you could to avoid using lethal force. Keep in mind that legal concepts like "stand your ground" and castle doctrine exist to protect those who righteously and appropriately defend themselves; *they are not there to expand opportunities for people to use defensive firearms.*

For a thorough legal education on the use of defensive force, I strongly encourage you to look into the Armed Citizens Legal Defense Network (www.armedcitizensnetwork.org). This organization is the best in the United States, when it comes to providing its members with accurate information about the laws and legal processes surrounding armed self-defense. It also provides legal assistance to its members and can help you find a qualified attorney in your area, should you need one after an incident or wish to consult with one before.

CHAPTER 14

IN THE WEEDS:

EXTREME CLOSE-QUARTERS SHOOTING

Defending yourself doesn't always "conveniently" happen at a measured five paces. These tips will help you survive when you're in the thick of it.

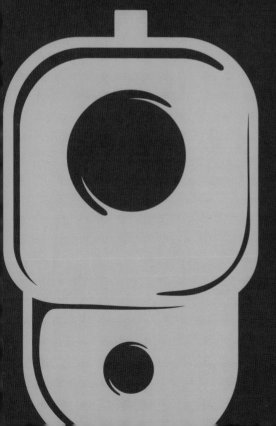

Your home is a confined space. Unlike defense in a public environment, and despite your efforts to remain out of reach, it is very possible that you will be in contact with your assailant, when you need to defend yourself from a lethal attack. That said, if you have a firearm, you need to think about shooting while in actual physical contact with your attacker.

When you have a firearm, when you have someone inside the space of a coat closet with you, someone who's pushed you down on the ground or is holding you against a wall, things are very different than they are at the shooting range. Now you're in a situation where you're in physical contact with someone and that someone isn't just a piece of paper. Real people are three dimensional, real people have energy. Real people are what your trying to defend yourself against, and real people put up a fight, have the means to hurt you, and will not simply let you shoot them as you perform the simple technique you practiced on a static target.

To get a better handle on dealing with an ultra-close encounter, let's look at a situation where someone is charging at you before you can bring your gun into your defensive action. In an extreme close-quarters situation such as this, as that threat comes in, you need to worry about deflecting that attack. You need to worry about protecting yourself from that screwdriver, knife, club, or other contact threat (such as hands in the case of, say, a large man coming at a small woman). As that knife comes in, your focus can't be to reach for your gun. Nor can your focus be to simply shove the

In an extreme close-quarters contact battle, when you are able to get your gun up and out of your holster, you'll want to keep the gun tight against your body while pointing it at your threat. The back of your strong-hand thumb and the magazine well should be jammed in your torso, both preventing you from pointing the gun at yourself while at the same time allowing the gun's slide to function.

bad guy away, nor even to strike him. If you do any of those things, you're almost certainly going to end up getting cut or stabbed as you put your hand out, and it's entirely possible you'll get knocked over. So what do you do? First and foremost, you need to worry about avoiding and controlling the attack. To do this, you need to focus on the "three Cs," in order: clear, control, and counter.

Here's how it should go with an attacker coming at you with a knife. Clear the knife from yourself or clear yourself from the knife, whatever is most efficient. Once you are clear of the initial threat, you need to work to control that threat. Maybe you isolate the attacker's knife hand by pushing it against a wall and hold it there. Now you can start to think about your defense, "countering" the attack.

If you're carrying a firearm, that counter is going to be a shot. That shot, that extreme close-quarters shot, is going to require a specific technique.

In the extreme close-quarters situation, if you have gotten to a point in the overall event where you are able to respond with your gun, you've already been actively involved in some type of fighting. You've cleared and controlled that initial attack, and now you're going to access my firearm. This moment is described by Craig Douglas, one of the top, close-quarters armed fighting instructors in the world, as "IFWA," or "in-fight weapons access." (Read more about this in the sidebar written by him in Chapter 11.). Maybe you're pinning your attacker against the wall, pinning him against the ground, controlling the knife, control-

WITHIN TWO ARMS' REACH

OUTSIDE 2 ARMS' REACH

Threat with contact weapon.

Clear. Control. Counter.

ling his head, *controlling him enough that you are confident you can get your firearm into a shooting position and use it without interruption or the risk of your attacker either defeating your ability to use it or taking it from you.*

When shooting while in contact, you'll want to get your firearm up and out of your holster and oriented right against your body, while pointing it at your threat. There are the two key components to this:

1. Get the magazine well jammed against your torso.
2. Get your strong-side thumb flagged against your torso.

These components, respectively, give you a very high likelihood of not having

Respond appropriately with defensive weapon.

the gun pointed at your own body and a very low likelihood of having your gun malfunction because the slide was not able to move freely.

There's another situation for extreme close-quarters shooting, wherein you might not actually be shooting while in contact. In this situation, if someone bursts through a door and you're in a very small room with your family behind you, you may not want to extend a handgun out into a normal shooting position and away from your body. If you go to full extension and your threat can reach out and touch your gun, they might be able to affect your aim, might be able to take your gun from you, jam the gun upwards or downwards, or affect you in other ways that prevent you being able to actually shoot and stop them (shoving your arm up and causing you to lose your balance, for instance). They could also cause the gun to malfunction.

Now take this situation and keep the gun in close, in the same position I described for shooting while in contact. What you need to take into consideration here is that you won't absolutely know that you're aligned on their body, because you won't be using the gun's sights. There is certainly the probability that you can hit an assailant from such a compressed shooting position, especially if you've practiced these kinds of shots, but you won't be as sure as you would be if you were in physical contact with your assailant.

The possibility of having to make such a shot lends itself to the use of a laser aiming device on your gun. In such a close-quarters but no contact assault, a laser aiming device is the most reliable way to know the alignment of your gun

Keeping your gun in close and tight to your body but oriented toward your threat can prevent you from accidentally shooting yourself during a close-contact battle, and it also helps minimize the possibility of your threat grabbing and gaining control of your defensive weapon.

on your intended target. For this reason, I often recommend a laser as a tertiary aiming device on a defensive handgun. When you're in extreme close quarters but not in contact, using a laser to aim the handgun is a great way to increase your ability to defend yourself or your family.

LONG GUN USE IN EXTREME CLOSE QUARTERS

If you've chosen to use a home-defense long gun, whether it's a rifle or a shotgun, and you get into an extreme close-quarters, shooting while in contact situation, defending yourself is going to be a lot harder than if you have a pistol. This is one of the reasons I say to people that, if you're really thinking you're going to be in a situation inside a home where you're going to need to move, where you're going to need to get family members together, and where you're going to do it while armed,

you are likely better off with a handgun. I'll be more specific than that: it should be a handgun in a holster.

With the handgun in the holster, if you get attacked at close quarters, you will respond as we've talked about, using the three Cs tactics. But, if all you have is a long gun, you may end up in a situation where they grab the gun, start to twist it, and eventually take it from you—and then you *really* have a problem. This is also one of the main reasons I never advise that, if you do insist on using a long gun as your primary home-defense weapon, you do not port it in a high ready position, where you have the muzzle of the firearm pointed up. Generally, you should have the stock of the long gun on your chest and the muzzle pointed *down* when you are not shooting, pointed just in front of your feet. If someone comes around the corner and grabs your gun when it's at high ready, unless you're a lot faster, a

The correct carry position for a long gun used in home-defense is one that has the muzzle pointed down, to a point in front of your feet. With the stock on your shoulder and the gun held close to you, It is the easiest position from which to get the gun into shooting position, and one that makes it hardest for your threat to grab and gain control of.

lot stronger, and a lot more skilled, you're at a huge disadvantage. When the muzzle is pointed up above the threat, you're not even going to be able to use the long gun as a firearm until you regain control of it. On the other hand, if you have a good low ready carry and someone comes around the corner and grabs it, at least you can use your torso and your momentum and energy to turn towards them and possibly get into a position to fire a shot into their foot or leg.

Optimally, you're not going to get into that situation at all. Optimally the gun's going to be kept compressed and the *stock* is going to be held high on your body (preferably by your strong hand). As you're moving forward through your home and if and when you are attacked at close quarters, you'll be able to keep this hand on the firearm. In the event of a close-quarters confrontation, you should then be able to pull the long gun back against your side, with the stock under your arm and the muzzle oriented towards your threat. Again, if you have a laser, you can use it to ensure alignment, though it will be more obvious where a rifle or shotgun is pointed in these circumstances, even without the aid of a laser.

CHAPTER 15

LIVING THE SINGLE (ROOM) LIFE

From hotel rooms to loft and studio apartments, at some point, most of us will find ourselves in a single-room dwelling. What are your options for self-defense when there's nowhere to go, nowhere to hide?

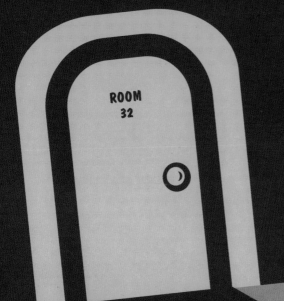

ROOM
32

Most of this book assumes that you live in a multi-room, possibly even multi-floor, home. In order to account for all the possibilities, both good and bad, that's the best approach for presenting this information. Obviously, though, if you don't have a second floor in your home, there's no need to worry about the stairwell references you find here. Similarly, if you live alone, you don't have to worry about the issues of other family members, but it would be a great failure if I were to address only single-person situations in a book about home-defense.

Generally, all the basic concepts laid out here apply regardless the home size—you don't have to live in the *Brady Bunch* house or the *Happy Days* home to apply the fundamentals. That said, if you live in a one-room efficiency or, like me, you spend much of your time in hotel rooms, there are some specific things you need to consider. Let's look at the advantages of these situations first.

The fact that there is only one entry point is something I see as an overall plus. For instance, you have only one door to spend money on to reinforce, if you are even able to do that. If you are renting, you may not be able to change/ upgrade the locks, but simple and effective barricade devices are available to help you secure this entry point. Floor-to-door bars that go around the door handle, and "barn door-style" horizontal bars that block the entire door and attach to the wall itself are easy and inexpensive options.

Another advantage is that even if you are on the "other side" of your home, you should be able to reach your staged defensive firearm very quickly in a single-room dwelling. In the same vein, and unlike it is with a large home having many different rooms, objects, and surfaces, it doesn't take much time to imagine a fight in a hotel room or efficiency apartment. With only one entrance, the angles of approach, barricade positions, and the likely angles and distances of your defensive shooting are very predictable. This means your plan will not have many variables.

Now for the disadvantages.

Evasion is not an option. Unless you were to somehow pass by your attacker as he came through the doorway, you are not going to be able to evade. Even if you are on the ground floor, for most people, climbing out a window is a cumbersome

Pack along a Wedge-It or other quality doorstop when traveling and secure a hotel-room door from unauthorized access. It's also a nice added measure of safety for other single-entry dwellings, like apartments and condos, and it certainly doesn't hurt to employ them on the last door to your barricade position.

action that takes time and leaves you extremely vulnerable. If you are half in and half out when the threat gets through the door, you are in a very compromised position. This means that you are much more likely to need to fight a home intruder than will someone who has more rooms to lock and/or hide in. In most hotel rooms and even the smallest apartments, you should remember that you might have the option of barricading in the bathroom.

The second disadvantage to single-room dwellings is that everything becomes extreme close-quarters fighting, and fighting within two arms' reach is different from fighting at further distances. If you are going to be within reach of the threat, you need to learn to shoot while in contact (discussed in Chapter 14). You are also more likely to

need to use unarmed fighting skills, like striking, blocking, and grappling.

Now that we've looked at the backdrop, how can you best set yourself up for success in a single room? First, you need to learn to fight in extreme close quarters. Even if you have plenty of warning that someone is coming in (because you have reinforced the door), that threat may cover the distance to you quickly, once they get through. Second, you need to have quick access to your defensive tool. Given that you are more likely to be alone in a hotel room or an efficiency apartment, or at least be less likely to have people in the space who are not authorized to access your firearms, you may consider having firearms that are unsecured, at least while you are home and awake. This makes it easier to get the firearm into your hand and prepped for use.

If you travel a significant amount of the time, you will probably want to invest in a couple of simple accessories. The first I recommend for a hotel room security enhancement is a quality doorstop. I recommend the Wedge-it, a plastic and rubber doorstop device that works on any inward opening door. You might even invest in two, knowing that you could move to barricade in the bathroom, if someone was trying to force their way in through the main door. These devices can be carried easily while you travel, even in your carry-on airline bag. You will also want a portable, quick-access safe, if you travel with a firearm. I usually travel with a GunVault Micro or Nano, and I often use them to secure firearms in my checked luggage, as well. You should choose a portable safe that has a cable for securing it to a permanent fixture in the hotel room, such as plumbing or a large piece of furniture.

Ultimately, whether your one-room setting is a hotel room, efficiency apartment, or even an office, you should be able to easily apply the fundamental concepts found in this book. While you have limited options in these environments, you should make that an advantage, rather than viewing such circumstances in their worst light.

The GunVault MicroVault (above) and NanoVault (left) slip easily into a messenger bag or knapsack. Either is perfect for transporting firearms in checked airline luggage. Both units also come with a steel cable that lets you secure the safe itself to a solid object.

CHAPTER 16

THE AFTERMATH:

WHAT HAPPENS AFTER YOU PULL THE TRIGGER?

Chaos doesn't stop once the bad guy's down.
How you deal with those moments immediately
after you've defended yourself and your family
can make the difference between your
life, death—and possibly jail time.

The immediate aftermath of an attack in your home is a critical time for which you need to plan ahead. It's something that often gets overlooked, when you think about your home-defense plan. Let's fix that.

IS HE REALLY DOWN? ARE THERE OTHERS?

When the bad guy comes into your house, you react and respond. If you need to use force, you put that bad guy down. Now you want to make sure your family is completely safe from the threat. If your family isn't right there with you, you'll probably want to go find those family members. If they are right there, you may be distracted by the thought of getting them away from the scene. While those are likely the first things you'll want to do, you need to remember that just because the bad guy's down doesn't necessarily mean that the fight is over.

An attacker that goes down, or an attacker that turns around and runs around a corner, isn't necessarily gone. Attackers sometimes come back, they sometimes get backup, and they sometimes have accomplices. Attackers who seem to flee might only run around the corner and stage another attack, or be waiting for you to see if you're going to come out of that bedroom or other barricade area, or even out of your house and make an attempt to get to a vehicle.

Are you thinking now? Just because an attacker's down doesn't mean you can let your guard down. You want to keep your firearm at the ready, you want to keep your eyes on that threat. *Don't approach the threat.* You do not need to

secure the intruder's weapon, you do not need to try to put someone into custody, so don't attempt to tie up or otherwise secure the threat. What you do need to do is keep your eyes on that threat, continue to try to contact law enforcement, and try to get out of the residence via a safe exit point if you can and take your family with you.

You also need to worry about multiple attackers. You may have only seen one bad guy, but it's possible there was another, one maybe coming in through another entrance or waiting out on your front porch, maybe even one who came in when he heard shots fired. Remember, multiple attackers are always possible.

STOP THE BLEEDING

The next things you want to worry about are medical issues. Were you injured? Was any member of your family injured? When you stage a phone, when you stage lights, defensive firearms, ammunition, body armor, whatever it is that you're actually staging, you also want to make sure you have medical equipment. Normal things like compression bandages should be included, and it might also be smart have a tourniquet and some type of hemostatic agent. The reality of it is that, if you are using force, you're probably defending yourself from a forceful attack and that attack could be successful against you. Indeed, that forceful attack might already have been perpetrated against you and your family by the time you're finally able to stop the threat. Medical assistance is something you should be at least as well-trained in as you are your

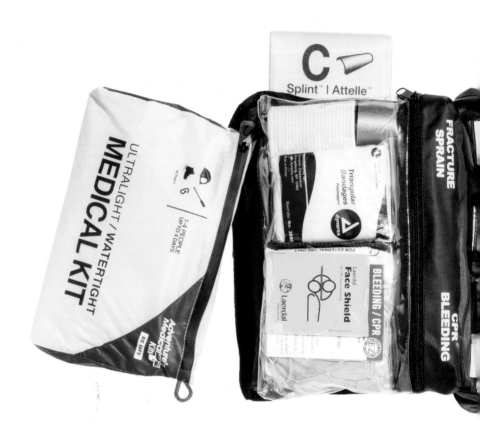

your defensive actions, when you think about a critical incident inside of your home. As you think about spending resources on training and equipment, this is another area that must be considered.

TALKING TO THE LAW

The first level of immediate aftermath is making sure the attack is really over. The second is medical care for yourself and your family, and the third should be an obvious issue:

dealing with law enforcement.

We've talked about the idea of how to deal with law enforcement when they come to you, you are in your barricade area, and you had no direct confrontation with the threat. You've got a firearm in your hand and you want to make sure *you* don't get shot, and also that you don't end up shooting a police officer when they're coming in to help you or your family. When it comes to dealing with responding police officers, you need to both cooperate with them

A thoroughly well-equipped first-aid kit should be part of your home no matter what, but, in terms of prepping for a home-defense situation, you'll likely want to add things like tourniquets and a hemostatic agent. You'll also want to have your kit located in your barricaded position, so you won't have to go looking for it—especially with a threat potentially still beyond your barricaded position—before the police have arrived and cleared the scene.

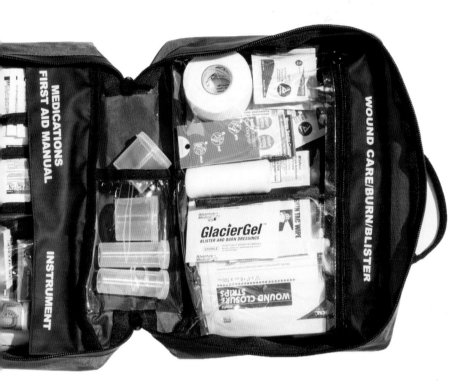

and make sure *they* know you are not a threat.

Once the attack is over and the guns are put away, you're going to find yourself being interviewed by the police. You might even find yourself being put into custody. *You might find yourself actually charged with a crime.*

Once those handcuffs are put on you and you are advised of your Miranda rights (including the very important right to remain silent) and actually told that you are being charged with a crime,

that's the time to stop talking. But, before those handcuffs get put on, or at least before you get formally arrested for a crime, that's the time you have to explain to the officer exactly what happened. There are several things you're going to want to explain at this point.

First, you want to make sure that the police understand that a crime was being perpetrated against you. If the officers come in and there's someone lying on the ground and you have a firearm in your hand and you fired shots into that person, the only crime they have obvious evidence of is you shooting another human being. So, you're going to need to point out things like, "Here's where they broke my window. Here's where they kicked in my door. There's their weapon," and so on. You're going to need to show damage that was done to you, and you're going to point out any injuries to a family member. This evidence of attack, the evidence of assault, the evidence of threat, the evidence of crimes perpetrated by the attacker, these are all things you need to point out during your initial interview with responding law enforcement. If you think there are witnesses to the crime, you also need to point them out. Maybe apartment dwellers on the other side of your shared wall were home and heard the screaming, heard you try to defend yourself and tell the guy to leave. Make sure the police talk to them.

However you do it, make sure that responding law enforcement understand there was a crime, there was a threat, there's evidence, there are witnesses—*you* are the best witness to explain that. The old cliché about not talking to the police may leave the police without the information they need to decide you acted appropriately and, so, decline to charge you with a crime. Remember these things in the immediate aftermath of an assault inside your home and make explaining them part of your home-defense drills.

PART II

HARDWARE
AND OTHER
CONSIDERATIONS

CHAPTER 17

HOME-DEFENSE HARDWARE:
CHOOSING THE RIGHT HANDGUN

The number of guns in the glass cases of your local gun shop can present a bewildering and intimidating cornucopia of choices. But, when it comes to home-defense, deciding which one is right for you is easily boiled down to a few fine points.

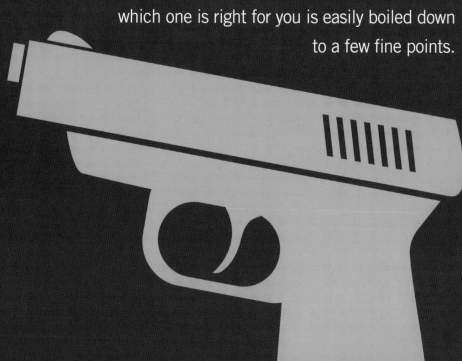

'm going to give you some tangible, objective information you can use when you head to the gun shop to purchase a defensive firearm, advice particularly suited to armed defense in the home. Overall, this will be a condensed primer on the topic of firearms selection, but one that will get you started in the right direction. I strongly recommend you seek out a knowledgeable defensive shooting instructor to guide you more specifically.

I'll be providing you a look at the best types of handguns, rifles, and shotguns. Let's get started with handguns and how to quickly and easily narrow down the mass of choices available.

RELIABILITY

Nothing is more important than reliability in your defensive firearm. Your gun *must* work.

The only way you can truly know if it will work is to take it to the range and test it. Test it with the ammunition that you intend to use in a defensive shooting and test it extensively, shooting it the way you believe you may have to when you are defending yourself or your family. After that, you must properly clean and maintain the firearm.

Ultimately, your firearm could still fail. The most reliable machines will breakdown and the highest quality ammunition can have a defect, but you have to stack the odds in your favor. A little research should go a long way. If you turn up dissenting opinions about a particular model's propensity to be reliable, I suggest you steer clear. It is one thing to have an anomaly or have someone be mistaken, but, if you have

an equal number of people telling you a type of gun is reliable as you do the other half telling you it isn't, take your search elsewhere. Your life isn't something you be flipping a coin over.

HANDGUN FIT

Beyond reliability, the initial factor you need to consider in your handgun choice is the fit. First and foremost, the firearm has to fit your hand. If the firearm you're going to use to defend yourself doesn't fit well in your hand, you're going to have to work harder than you should need to, in order to use it.

You want to make sure you can get a solid, full grip on the firearm. To do this, you need to be able to have the web of your hand between the thumb and index finger directly behind the gun, so that your thumb knuckle is beside the gun, not under the back of the frame. The axis of the movement of the slide should be aligned with your wrist, when you are at extension.

Make sure your index finger can comfortably reach the trigger, while your hand is in this position. Much discussion occurs about the best connection between your trigger finger and the trigger, but you really shouldn't overthink it. For defensive shooting, anywhere on the pad of the tip of your finger is good, though, if it is the inward half of the pad, the area closer to the first knuckle is all the better.

You want to make sure you can hold the firearm so that there's no gap above your hand relative to the top of the grip area, in order to help you manage recoil. A proper grip in this manner is important to the physics of the gun being reliable and also provides you the capability of delivering a rapid string of fire efficiently.

Head to any public range and you will see some people cheating their hand one way or the other so that they can reach the trigger. This puts them in a bad physical relationship with the gun. It also indicates that the gun doesn't fit their hand. There are so many guns available in so many shapes and sizes that it's ridiculous for any adult with a fully formed and functioning hand to have to compromise their handgun fit. Many of the recommended defensive firearms even have different sizes within one model line, and many now have interchangeable grip panels or backstraps to make them customizable.

Don't be fooled by your (or someone else's) ability to shoot well without a good grip, when you're shooting in a controlled, target range environment. Many of my students (and those attending other schools) have come to a two- or three-day defensive shooting class, spending a lot of money to do so. In some cases, thousands of dollars are spent to attend such classes, including that for tuition, ammunition, travel, food, etc. When that kind of money is being spent, it's fairly easy for me to say to one of my students, "Hey, that gun doesn't fit your hand. Get one that does."

Physical comfort is also important for students in a shooting class. You must be able to do whatever it is I'm teaching and, if your gun doesn't fit your hand, it will affect how well you can perform the skills you are trying to

learn. In extreme cases, it makes some skills impossible to accomplish.

For my regular students, losing $100 in a trade for a gun that better fits them or having to spend an extra $50 for a more accommodating holster is a small price to pay for huge gains in efficiency. Still, I have to acknowledge that some people are forced to carry a specific firearm. For instance, when I get military personnel sent to me and they're carrying their issue handgun and it doesn't fit their hand, we work around it to find solutions. If you're in the military, law enforcement, in a particular line of private security work, or possibly on a very limited budget, you may not have the option of switching from one gun to another. Find a solution and make it work.

ACTION TYPES—GO MODERN

I've addressed the strong side and the back of the gun in regards to how the gun fits in your hand, and now I want to examine the weak side of the gun. I don't recommend any firearm that has extra levers or buttons beyond the trigger, a slide-lock lever, and a magazine release. If your gun has a manually operated external safety or a decocker, it's just not the most efficient design available for your personal-defense or your armed professional use.

The type of handgun I advocate for defensive use is the modern striker-fired gun. These types of firearms are reliable and affordable. They have a moderate trigger pull weight and length, and the applicable models tend to sit low in the hand, which means they are easier to align on your target and shoot rapidly.

Modern striker-fired
handguns like the
Smith & Wesson
M&Ps shown here are
reliable and efficient.

If you're not choosing a modern striker-fired gun for personal-defense, there needs to be a compelling reason why you would be carrying a gun that is inherently more complicated and, therefore, less efficient. It takes more time, effort, and energy to learn how to proficiently use a more complicated gun; there are more opportunities for failure when you're using a more complicated gun in an ambush moment. Operating such handguns also requires finer motor skills (even extra motor skills), and that sets you up for more potential failure in an armed home-defense moment.

The three models of modern striker-fired guns I recommend most often are Glocks (Models 17, 19, 26, or 34), S&W Military & Police (full-size or compact in 9mm), and the Springfield Armory XD or XD-M (full-size or compact in 9mm). Over the years, I've found these guns to be extremely reliable and efficient as handled by a wide variety of students. The reason I recommend 9mm handguns for defense is that the 9mm round gives the least amount of recoil, has the highest capacity (in any given gun size), and the ammunition can be purchased at the lowest cost of all the modern rounds that meet the minimum recommended level of power for stopping a threat.

Outside of modern striker-fired semi-automatic handguns, you will find three major options: single-action pistols, double-/single-action pistols, and double-/single-action revolvers. Let's look at each type a little closer.

Single-action semi-auto pistols utilize early 1900s-era technology and design and are characterized by their very short

Times have changed. Handguns with extra levers (like the safety on this single-action-only seen here), are more complicated than the many striker-fired pistols available today. Simply put, extra levers like manual safeties and decockers take extra motor skills, extra learning, and extra practice, and lacking any of these can set you up for failure when you're in a real-life self-defense situation.

and crisp triggers. These types of handguns and triggers are known for extreme precision capabilities. Indeed, this type of pistol remains popular among a wide variety of shooters, but this is more due to the design's traditional aspects (think Colt's 1911 and Browning's Hi-Power), their long and storied histories, and the large number of companies producing dozens of variations on these designs, than it is the design's inherent defense capabilities.

Remember, however, that you are not likely to need what a firearms enthusiast would consider an extreme level of precision, when you're in the middle of a home-defense event. Any advantage given by the short, crisp trigger on a single-action gun is offset by the need to use a manually operated, external safety lever. In other words, it requires you perform an extra action before the gun can be fired.

Still, many people initially believe that a safety on a firearm is an advantage, but I would challenge you to experience proper defensive firearms instruction and shooting before you chose that option. If you are storing your firearms responsibly and controlling access to them, I would be more concerned about that manual safety hampering your ability to use the firearm when you need it, than I would be expecting it to prevent an accident.

Double-/single-action semi-auto pistols are products of the mid-1900s and feature the most complicated design available; some would say they offer both the best and worst of all other

Springfield Armory's XD striker-fired 9mm is one of the author's top picks for a defensive handgun. With its simple and reliable operation, it's easy to learn on, and the high grip helps keep recoil and followup shots manageable.

handgun designs in one convenient package. With this type of firearm, you have a trigger that is long and heavy (double-action) when you fire the first shot, making it relatively hard to control. After that first shot, you have a short, crisp trigger (single-action) for all your follow-up shots. When you are done shooting a string of fire, you then must use a de-cocking lever to put the trigger back into the safer double-action mode. If all that weren't enough to learn, some decocking levers also serve as manually operated external safeties. A final negative aspect of the DA/SA pistol design is that, because of the exposed hammer design, the barrel sits relatively high above the hand, making it less intuitive to align on your target, as well as harder to shoot quickly.

On the other hand, today's modern double-/single-action *revolvers* are an older handgun design that can be used productively for home-defense. (The single-action-only revolvers reminiscent of the Old West are not a practical option for the issues of home invasion and home-defense addressed in this book.) Revolvers are very reliable, though they do have a long, heavy trigger and relatively low capacity compared to most semi-auto pistols. For many decades, revolvers have been recommended to people who were new to shooting, because of their inherent simplicity of operation. They are definitely easy to load (as long as you are not trying to go quickly), and they are simple to shoot (as long as you can get a good grip and manage the trigger weight). Still, they are not my first recommendation for a home-defense firearm.

Why? Several reasons. First, as I said, they have a relatively low capacity, usually six (sometimes eight in some calibers, many of which are smaller and not the best choice for home-defense). Compare that to the 12 to 18 rounds available in a typical, modern, 9mm semi-automatic of similar size. Second, revolvers, being hammer-fired guns, have a high bore axis, which can make target alignment and recoil management more difficult. Finally, they have challenging triggers. (For more information on the special nature of revolvers, see the section at the end of this chapter, where Certified Combat Focus Shooting Instructor and world-renown revolver-smith Grant Cunningham, who has literally written the book on defensive revolvers—see his books, *Defensive Revolver Fundamentals* and *Gun Digest Book of the Revolver,* available at www.gundigeststore.com—has graciously provided his expert thoughts.)

Now that you understand the options, let's get back to the fit of the gun. Hopefully, the only buttons or levers you will need to worry about using regularly are the trigger and the magazine release. As noted above, some handguns have safety levers and decockers; even some modern striker fired handguns come equipped with manually operated, external safety levers. (If you have one of those, you need to learn how to use it properly and factor its location and size into your selection of a handgun.) You want to make sure the firearm fits in your hand so that you can use the trigger properly, and also so you can hit the magazine release efficiently for reloading purposes. Make an adjustment or a different choice in gun if this isn't the case for you. For instance, I shoot Glocks more often than any other gun, but I cannot hit the magazine release conveniently. Because of this, I generally install an extended magazine release on my Glocks.

The extended/oversized magazine releases are one of the few modifications to defensive guns that are often a good idea. Ensuring that your trigger finger can touch the trigger and that your thumb can hit the magazine release without changing your grip on the gun are very important components of how your handgun fits. If you find a gun that fits you well for shooting and requires only minimal movement of the hand around the gun as you release the magazine during a reload, you can often develop a method for making that movement without losing any time on your reload. If, on the other hand, you are forced to make a gross change in the position of your grip or use your weak hand to release the magazine, you should change guns.

The other lever you will find on most modern defensive and striker-fired guns is a slide-lock (or, on older guns, a slide-release) lever. This lever allows you

Many compact firearms, like this Glock, will accept the magazines from their larger versions in the same caliber. This allows you to have a gun you can carry conveniently, yet still have the capacity of a larger gun in a home-defense situation.

to pull the slide back and lock the gun open (This function is for the purposes of clearing a malfunction, cleaning, putting it away, etc.). Again, it is best if you can operate this part without shifting your grip.

In summary, there are three things necessary for your defensive gun to be a good fit:

- You must be able to actuate the trigger.
- You must be able to actuate the magazine release.
- You must be able to actuate the slide-lock in the event of a malfunction.

If you can't do those three things with a particular gun, then the gun does not fit your hand. If you happen to be stuck with a gun that has extra levers or buttons, you still want to be able to use them with little or no change of your hand position on the gun. For instance, being able to run either a safety lever or a decocker with your strong hand thumb, but without shifting your grip, will be important for your efficiency and consistency.

THE ARGUMENT FOR GOING 9MM

Why do I not recommend a larger caliber for a home-defense handgun, like a .40-caliber or a .45-caliber? I have several reasons.

The first reason is that there is only a small difference in the wounding capacity between a 9mm and a .40-caliber. In fact, trauma doctors I've spoken with who actually deal with gunshot wounds in hospitals are hard-pressed to tell the difference between any of the median-caliber bullets (.380, 9mm, .38 Special, .357 Magnum, .40-caliber, .357 SIG, 10mm, and .45-caliber). It's very hard for doctors to discern caliber difference by looking at a wound. In fact, I haven't found any doctor who says they can reliably tell the difference between a wound caused by a .40-caliber and one by a 9mm. I haven't spoken to every doctor on earth, but I am confident of my findings, due to the fact that there is only a single millimeter difference between a 9mm bullet and a .40-caliber bullet (a .40-caliber is a 10mm bullet).

Although the wounding capacities are essentially the same, there are also other important factors that play into my

Because the shooter has the ability to manage the recoil of the 9mm much more efficiently than they can other, larger calibers, much more damage can be done to the assailant's body in the same amount of shooting time. In other words, and simply put, you can shoot faster with a 9mm.

recommendation. The primary reason I recommend a 9mm over a .40-caliber is recoil management. But before I talk about why recoil management is so important, I need to give you some context.

Many years ago, there was a body of research that became popular and created a trendy idea in the gun community called "the one-shot stop." The idea of the one-shot stop has really faded from popularity in the research and training community at this point, but the idea is still floating around out there. Frankly, the one-shot stop is a mostly a myth,

PHOTO COURTESY VOLK

Virtually any reliable 9mm handgun that you can operate efficiently is going to be a great home-defense option.

and even whatever truth may exist has a lot of gray area. Let me illustrate.

If someone armed with a big knife were to burst into my room right now and I had a firearm, I would draw and shoot right away. It takes little to no imagination to assume that, if I shot in his direction and he had only a knife, he would turn around and run for his life. However, for the purpose of this discussion, let's say that I have fired one shot and it was a direct hit. After being shot and going into shock, he turns and runs 300 yards down the block, takes a right, runs another 100 yards, hides in some bushes, and the police find him bled out and dead three hours later.

By definition, that counts as a one-shot stop. The hole in the logic of that conclusion is that it wasn't a physiological stop. It wasn't the actual, physiological damage that the bullet instantly did in the intruder's body that caused him to drop the knife and stop his attack. He didn't fall down lifeless from my one shot. Indeed, he ran away out of fear and shock—but you have to know that, instead of running away, the perpetrator could have used all his energy to come at me, violently swinging his knife. So, even though this kind of situation would have qualified as a "one-shot stop" by some standards, it's clear there were many more factors involved than my one shot before my attacker died.

Once you understand that a single pistol bullet has relatively low wounding potential and that one shot is not likely going to stop an attacker, it no longer makes sense to compare individual pistol bullet sizes. History and experience would suggest that one round of fire is neither sufficient nor guaranteed to completely incapacitate an assailant. Thus, planning for multiple

Modern 9mm hollowpoint rounds with bonded jackets consistently achieve the type of performance needed from a defensive bullet.

shots is absolutely necessary. So, if you need to plan on firing multiple shots in a personal-defense situation, physics say you can fire a 9mm round faster than you can fire a .40-caliber round, a .357 SIG round, or a .45-caliber round.

That brings us back to the main reason I recommend a 9mm bullet: recoil management. Obviously, the size, weight, and grip of the gun play their roles in your personal performance, but regardless those factors, you can still fire a 9mm bullet faster than any other caliber, all because of physics.

This is not a guaranteed, scientific number, but let's say that a .40-caliber bullet has 10-percent more practical wounding capacity than a 9mm bullet. Within the first second of shooting each of these calibers side by side, naturally, the speed at which either is fired is equal. However, as time increases and physics come into play, the ratio changes. For example, let's say you can fire three 9mm rounds and three .40-caliber rounds in one second. Seems equal, right? However, by the time you reach one and a half seconds, you're able to fire five of the 9mm rounds, but can fire only four of the .40-caliber rounds. Because you can fire the 9mm measurably faster as more seconds pass, you are capable of firing more total rounds within a given amount of time. Now, if the .40-caliber bullet only has a 10-percent damage advantage over the 9mm bullet, it's easy to see how being able to fire more 9mm rounds in the same amount of time will not only make up the difference, but will actually overcome it. Once you get to two seconds, you've fired five .40-caliber rounds and

are likely up to seven 9mm rounds. You get to two and a half seconds, and the ratio turns from seven to 10 rounds in favor of the 9mm.

Because the shooter has the ability to manage the recoil of the 9mm much more efficiently, much more damage can be done to the assailant's body in the same amount of time. Yes, shot placement and accuracy are important factors, but, if you are firing many more shots into your target, your chances of hitting a vital organ or artery are much higher. No matter how you look at it, the 9mm has the potential to break down the bad guy's body much faster than a larger-caliber bullet, simply because of recoil management.

It is important to note that this is something I have changed my mind about over the years. (In fact, it is very important to admit that I've changed my mind about a lot of things over the years! If you know an instructor who

The Steyr company makes a line of reliable striker-fired handguns. Although the stock triangular-shaped front sight is unorthodox, it does stick to the traditional notch-and-blade concept.

can't admit that, I suggest you find a new instructor.) If you had asked me about defensive handguns 20 years ago, I would have told you that 1911-style single-action pistols were the way to go, if you were serious about personal-defense, and that .45-caliber bullets were the only caliber that existed. Then, in the mid-'90s, I had my first serious look at modern striker-fire guns, when I discovered the Glock 23. That gun held 14 total rounds of .40-caliber bullets, which was the new, cool, hip round, and its popularity was underscored by the fact that law enforcement agencies were switching to it in droves. I could even carry 14 rounds of .40 versus six, seven, or eight rounds of .45.

At the time, I was also starting to understand the mechanical issues of working the pistol's safety under stress and seeing the advantages of getting

rid of some of those extra levers and buttons. I bought into the .40 in every way and heavily invested in it. I recommended it, and I personally owned a lot of .40-caliber guns in that era (I still own them, but, now, many have 9mm conversion barrels in them).

I'm not the only one who has been reevaluating the old "bigger is better" approach. As I was writing this book, many law enforcement agencies, including the FBI, have switched or are seriously considering switching back to the 9mm, after years of carrying .40s and larger caliber sidearms.

I used to teach that, if you were in a firefight, the most important thing was to hit your target first, even if that meant shooting before you were fully extended into a shooting position. What I've come to realize since then, especially with the development of

Though this Ruger .380 might be an acceptable choice for low-profile concealed carry, it is not a recommended option for home-defense.

9mm hollowpoints, is that the most important thing in a firefight is to be the *last* person to fire shots into the target. There is no race to see who can fire first; there is a race to see who can fire last. I don't want to take two seconds to fire five shots, when it could take me just one and a half seconds.

The ease with which you can manage the recoil of a 9mm allows you to fully extend into proper shooting position and fire more shots into your attacker than a higher caliber bullet in the same amount of time. That, *that* is the primary reason I recommend the modern 9mm for personal-defense.

Another noteworthy point is that many defensive situations involve multiple threats. Being able to shoot multiple rounds into multiple assailants is another reason you would want a high-capacity caliber. Obviously, because of their size, larger-caliber guns hold fewer rounds in their magazines than do 9mm guns. No matter what the situation is, the more rounds you can carry in a personal-defense gun the better. Thus, the 9mm comes out ahead again.

The last factor I want to touch on is the least exciting point, but it is one that's incredibly practical and beneficial. The fact of the matter is that 9mm rounds are less expensive than any other commonly recommended caliber. This, naturally, implies that your budget will allow you to train more frequently and realistically with 9mm rounds than you could with .40 or .45 rounds. You can't short-change the larger calibers in this context: If you carry a .45 but train with a 9mm, your training suffers because it is less realistic. Likewise, if you carry a .45 and shoot less frequently to save money on .45 ammo costs, your training suffers and your results will show it. And so there you have the final reason I highly recommend a 9mm caliber, because it affords most people the opportunity to train more frequently and realistically.

Being able to shoot multiple rounds into multiple assailants is sound reason for having a gun in a caliber that enables high capacity. No matter what the situation, the more rounds you can carry in a personal-defense gun the better.

Special Considerations for Revolvers in Home-Defense

By Grant Cunningham

Many people choose a revolver for home-defense, and for some very good reasons, but there are some special considerations when it comes to using one as a home-defense tool.

On the plus side of the ledger, one of the areas where the revolver shines has to do with its tolerance for neglect. A gun that's staged for home-defense, as opposed to one that's carried on your person daily and relegated to the bedroom in the evenings, may go for long periods of time without being fired, cleaned, or lubricated. Many people have plucked old revolvers out of nightstand drawers, guns that hadn't been fired for decades, and they still operated perfectly and without any extra attention. It's tough, if not impossible, to find an auto-loader that would happily endure the same treatment!

All that said, there are some serious considerations to be made, when choosing a revolver for home-defense. The first is caliber. The magnum cartridges for which many revolvers are chambered are not usually a good choice for home-defense. Those cartridges are much more difficult to control in strings of fire, and strings of fire are likely what you'll be shooting when faced with a threat. That difficulty in control negatively impacts the balance between speed and precision.

I know, I know, you're really good with magnums and believe you shoot them very well. Fact is, though, no matter how good you are with a magnum, you will be better with a +P Special, and yet will give up no statistically valid amount of effectiveness.

Still not convinced? Consider that the blast and noise that emanate from a magnum is severe in close quarters. If you've never experienced it, you need to get to a practice shoot-house with rooms of size similar to yours at home and try them out. I've seen very proficient shooters who shoot magnum revolvers in such simulators and immediately develop a severe flinch, even with good hearing protection! Unprotected ears, which is what yours will be in a home invasion situation, will most certainly be damaged by the extreme report of a couple magnum rounds fired in a bedroom, and more rapidly and assuredly than is likely with a non-magnum version of the same caliber.

That brings me to my second point, which is the need to fit your guns to everyone in your household who will have access to them. Even if you are the greatest magnum speed shooter who ever lived, how likely is it that the other people authorized to use that gun in defense of the home are as capable as you? Pick the cartridge that the least well-trained of your group can control in realistic strings of fire (three to five rounds).

Whether it's just you or the need to address a household of potential users (keeping in mind the capabilities of the least well-trained), part of choosing the right firearm/s has to be done with recoil control in mind. For instance, the extremely lightweight titanium and scandium alloy revolvers are punishing, even with .38 Special +P rounds, and most non-dedicated shooters find them difficult, if not impossible, to adequately and reliably control. If you're going to pick a revolver, it's probably best to focus on steel-framed models that will mitigate the effects of recoil on the shooter. After all, gun weight shouldn't be a big problem for a firearm that's going to be stored in a quick-access safe (as opposed to carried on your body).

Controlability by all potential users in your house isn't the only concern. The gun also needs to be sized for the smallest authorized hands in the house. Since revolvers are more flexible in this regard than are auto-loaders, you should be able to find a combination of frame and grip sizes that will accommodate everyone. Indeed, it's far easier for you to shoot a gun that's a little too small for your hands than it is one that's too big. Beyond hand fit, also make sure that the gun is balanced well enough for everyone to be able to index it on target. A six-inch barreled revolver looks great and shoots like a million bucks from a bench, but, for many people, such a long barrel is difficult to hold on target when a rest isn't available. Stick to the shorter-barreled guns, four inches and under, unless everyone who will use it is capable of handling the extra weight of a longer barrel and bigger overall gun.

If hand strength is an issue with some members of the family, consider even more carefully the choice of the revolver. I've counseled hundreds of men who decided they needed a revolver for home-defense, because their partner was petite and had little upper body and hand strength. The usual belief is that such a person can't rack the slide of an autoloader, and so it's assumed that the revolver would be easier to handle. That's usually not the case. In situations where someone has trouble with the autoloader's heavy recoil spring as it relates to manipulating the slide, they almost always also have trouble with the revolver's much heavier trigger. The big difference is that racking a slide on a semi-auto can easily be done with proper technique, but there is no such compensation for the trigger finger and heavy trigger weight.

POLICE BULLDOG .38 SPL.

If you have someone in the house whom you feel cannot rack the slide of an auto-loader, instead of defaulting to the revolver, it's better to teach them the various techniques for racking the slide. Better yet, find an instructor who understands what to do and have them teach the family member. It won't take long. With proper instruction, most people who thought they could never operate a stiff slide are chambering and clearing the gun with no problem inside of a minute. I know it sounds a bit counter-intuitive, but an auto-loading pistol is actually often the better choice for someone with a strength issue.

Remember that it's plausible you'll need to shoot a revolver one-handed. For instance, you might have the phone or a flashlight in your supporting hand, when the need to shoot presents itself. Because of that long, heavy, double-action trigger, you'll find the revolver much harder to shoot with just the one hand. It's going to take practice and a focus on good grasp and trigger control to make the same kinds of hits you make easily with two hands on the same gun. But the difference between one-handed and two-handed

shooting with a revolver tends to be much greater than the difference when performing the same shooting using the shorter, lighter triggers of the auto-loader, so you'll need to spend extra time to practice these skills with a revolver.

Finally, if you carry and train with an auto-loader most of the time, you're going to need to devote extra practice resources to that revolver sitting locked in your bedroom. That revolver is harder to shoot and requires more dedication to get the same results you get easily with your semi-auto. Make sure you make the time to shoot it occasionally, to the point you can get roughly the same results as you do with your other gun.

The upside to extra practice with a revolver is that you'll probably find your results with the semi-auto will improve, but the opposite is not as universally true. There are reasons for this, which we don't have space to consider here, but it's a phenomenon that's been reported widely for many years. When you go to the range, make sure you take that home-defense revolver with you, too, and make sure to practice realistically.

Revolvers can be a good home-defense tool, but you should understand their shortcomings and be sure to practice with one, if you choose to go that route.

CHAPTER 18

GET A GRIP!
(A DEFENSIVE HANDGUN GRIP, THAT IS!)

Skin to gun, hands on high. Perfect your gun grip and intuitive shooting will come to the aid you when there's no time for the sights.

The reason I want to spend some time focusing specifically on your handgun grip is that, honestly, your grip on a rifle or shotgun is much less important. The nature of those tools makes getting a good enough grip very intuitive (though stance is another issue). The very term handgun reveals the importance of how your hands interact with the tool. While how to get the best grip on your handgun may not be obvious, it is truly an easy thing to master, once you understand the important parts of a proper grip and have a gun that fits you well.

The primary function of the grip is to create and maintain control of the gun during shooting and recoil. Because the mechanism of control is actually friction

The web of your strong hand needs to be up as high as it can be against the sweep of the top of the pistol's backstrap.

between your hand and the gun, you want to get as much contact on the gun as you can in order to manage recoil. This also helps you to get as much tactile feedback as possible, telling you your hands are or are not in the correct place. Further, the more of your skin that touches the gun and the more your hands are touching each other, the more consistency you'll have when you grip your gun.

Consistency is the major factor here. The more consistent your points

Having your thumbs layered and not crossed in any way means that you will have as much flesh as possible on the gun to help manage recoil. Such a grip will also ensure consistency for your strong hand during both one-handed and two-handed shooting.

of contact are with the gun, the more your brain will recognize that you're in the correct position to shoot, the more accurate and efficient you'll be and the easier it will be for you to handle your gun. If you want to be able to rely on

kinesthetic alignment of the gun (more on that in a bit) to put rounds into a threat under the most probable situations, you need consistency. Anyone can hit with a sloppy grip if they use the sights, but a solid grip is required

When shooting at your threat's chest area from close range, the gun should be extended fully and parallel and in line with your line of sight, with your vision focused on the target.

PHOTO COURTESY VOLK

to shoot intuitively and perfect fast follow-up shots. More friction on the gun means better recoil management, and more points of contact means more consistency.

I recommend a high grip on the gun. It keeps your trigger finger somewhere above the trigger area when you're not shooting (great for safety), and positions your middle finger up against the bottom of the triggerguard. There should be no gap at the back of the gun between the top of the web of your hand and the gun's beavertail. In other words, hold the gun as high as possible in all areas, so that the mass of your hand is as close as it can be to the action of the slide.

Next, create a big gap on the weak side of the gun by holding your thumb high. Then, place the meaty part of your weak hand at the base of the thumb and palm and place it in that gap. Get as much contact as you possibly can without crossing your thumbs. There should be no part of the frame of the gun visible between your strong and weak hands; you want your thumbs to be layered. Next, wrap the fingers of your weak hand around the front of the gun, on top of the fingers of your strong hand (they should, basically, be parallel with the strong-hand fingers). Keep your index finger in contact with the bottom of the triggerguard. This grip will create as much friction as possible on the gun and between your hands.

CHAPTER 19

TAKE YOUR BEST POSITION:
DEFENSIVE SHOOTING POSTURES

Leave the Weaver and isosceles stances at the range (or behind altogether, if you're not a bull's-eye competitor). You need different gun handling skills, when you're barricaded in a corner of your bedroom.

As I did with the chapter on handgun grip, I'm going to take a special section of the book just to deal with a handgun issue. Unlike a rifle or shotgun, which provide up to four points of contact between it and you—control hand, support hand, cheek, and torso—to create proper alignment, a handgun has only one point of contact. Yes, one: while you may have two hands on the gun, they are in the same place. Therefore, you need to be much more specific in your handgun shooting grip and position, in order to align the gun properly on your target. (In fact, the main advantage of long guns, when it comes to home-defense, is the very fact that it is almost always going to be easier to get hits with them.) I've discussed how to get a proper grip on your handgun, now let's integrate that with how you'll use the rest of your body to best address a lethal home-defense situation.

FULL ARM EXTENSION

Reaching full extension with both arms is the best way to increase both your ability to manage recoil and achieve the consistency with which you position the handgun relative to your line of sight. But full extension when shooting means more than just making sure your arms are straight (though without hyperextending the elbow).

There are theories floating around out there that suggest your hands or arms can somehow "absorb" the recoil if they are not fully extended during a string of fire. The flaws in this line of thought are nearly innumerable.

The physics of a modern, semi-automatic firearms require the frame of the

pistol remain unmoving, relative to the slide. In order for the gun to do what it's supposed to do, the frame must maintain its position in space, while the slide moves fully back and forward. As the slide moves back, the recoil spring compresses and stores energy. At the same time, the empty case is pulled, by the extractor, out of the chamber and back against the ejector. The ejector is attached to the frame, therefore, that frame needs to be stable so that the ejector pushes the case out of the way of the next round coming up out of the magazine and moving into the chamber. After the slide's full movement backward, the slide, via the stored energy in the re-coil spring, can then return forward with as much force as possible, stripping the next round from the magazine and fully seating it into the chamber.

Of course, there are other mechanical things happening at the same time to reset the trigger (movement and interaction of springs, levers, hammers, strikers, etc.). All that stuff has to reset every time the gun is fired, and the mechanical elements of the gun benefit from the frame being held as still as possible while in use. This isn't meant to be a gunsmithing book, but it's important to understand how the basic mechanics of the gun work, so that your technique can actually help it perform at its highest potential.

If at any point you absorb recoil at one of your joints, whether it's in your elbows, shoulders, hips, or wrists, it is possible you are contributing to an *unsupported platform failure*. The old terminology that used to refer to this was "limp-wrist" fail-ure. Any unsupported platform, anything you do that lets the frame move, is bad. So, when I hear people talk about letting your arms act as shock absorbers, I cringe. Even if the gun's reliable in the moment of moving at the elbows, it's still harder to shoot faster, because you have more work to do to get the gun back where it needs to be for the next shot and the next and the next. If you bend your elbows, the gun is moving in two planes as it moves backwards and up, and this makes it much harder to track and get back on target. It should be obvious that movement at the wrist would produce the same effect. Too, if you put your shoulders right over your hips, you have the potential for full body movement backwards, and this is true even if your arms are straight.

A student of the Combat Focus® Shooting Program, Paul DiRenzo, is a very accomplished martial arts instructor and fitness coach. When I was writing on this topic for my book *Counter Ambush*, I realized he actually understood a bit more about the science of why an extended position helps so much with consistency and stability. After training with several of our instructors for more than six months, and after having the chance to observe many students in our recommended shooting position, he offered an explanation for why it works

so well. Paul told me, "By bending the knees, you actively engage all the major muscles groups south of your belt line. The calves, hamstrings, quads, and glutes are all in an active working state to keep you vertical and allow you to put your body weight forward into the action."

The really important stuff is happening above the hips. By actively leaning forward through the midsection (imagine pushing your chest into a wave), you tell your body to recruit the muscles of its core, in order to brace against the impact. The transverse abdominis muscle tightens to stabilize the spinal column, and the obliques and the rectus muscles (your six-pack muscles) engage and flex in order to pull your upper body forward to lean into the position.

Paul explained, "With your upper body, the chest and shoulder muscle groups are what move the arms into an extended position. Muscles are at their strongest in the middle of their range of motion, so, the pectoral muscles should be at roughly 75 percent of flexion, as should be the muscles of the triceps (it's like as it would be at the top third of a push-up). That's the easy part, because, again, that's where your muscles are at their strongest

When you drive your gun out in front of you, you want your shoulders locked forward. This will mean that the recoil of the gun, through the frame, is pushing back against your torso, and all that musculature will be working to make sure that your gun's frame doesn't move any more than necessary.

position. Also working to hold the body and create a position of stabilization are the wide muscles of the back (latissimus and dorsi), the biceps, the forearm flexors and extensors, and even the neck."

Without your shoulders actively engaged and forward of the torso, you can't engage the back and neck muscles. The more muscles you have involved, the more kinesthetic consistency will be involved. Of course, you can't count on being in a standing position when you need to defend yourself, so *the most important aspect of your defensive shooting position is full extension of the arms and shoulders, placing the gun in and parallel with your line of sight.* This can happen even if you are on the ground or seated.

Picture an Olympic weight lifter. They pick up and lift weights over their head, but they don't complete their lift with their shoulders kind of loose and their arms out to their side. They set their shoulders up above their shoulder blades and torso. The shoulders aren't out to the side with their arms straight; their shoulders are *engaged over their torso* to support the maximum amount of weight.

This is how you want your gun extension to be. When you drive your gun out in front of you, you want your shoulders locked forward (just as the weight lifter locks his when his arms are up and the barbell is overhead). This will mean that the recoil of the gun, through the frame, is pushing back against your torso. All the musculature described by Paul will be working to make sure that the frame doesn't move anymore than is necessary.

The best part of all this is that this position, the one that is best to support the physics of the gun, is also congruent with

what happens when you're startled. When you're startled, you lower your center of gravity, closing down at the hips, leaning forward, and bending your knees. You're *naturally* in a position that facilitates support to the gun's frame. In this manner, when you draw your gun and drive it out, you will be in a natural position during a fight and, so, you form the strongest possible platform for the firearm.

KINESTHETIC ALIGNMENT

"Kinesthetic alignment" is the most efficient way to align any gun, when it is in the shooting position. By consistently engaging in the recommended grip and the recommended extended shooting position, you can actually learn to feel when the gun is in the right position.

A simpler definition of kinesthetic alignment is that of simply combining your awareness of the position of your body parts with your ability to interact with a tool consistently. In the case of gun handling, such alignment and awareness will work to put the gun in the same place every time.

SIGHTS OR NO SIGHTS? BOTH!

Understand that what I've just been talking about is *unsighted* fire. Intuitive, unsighted fire involves full extension parallel with the line of sight, with the final motion of the gun being pushed forward, so that you achieve full muscle engagement behind the frame of the gun.

If you have any doubt that you can do this very easily, think about any sport that involves a racquet, bat, or club. Think about the last time you drove a nail with a hammer. For instance, even if you haven't ever actually played tennis, I'm sure you've

seen other people play the game on TV or in person. Have you ever seen a tennis player look down at the racket and check a bubble level as the ball is flying towards them? Have you ever seen them check a little laser protractor to verify that the racket head is at the angle of alignment that will get the ball back across the net? Have you ever seen a tennis player take their eye off the ball to check anything on their racquet during live play? Of course not! Through frequent and realistic training, they have learned to interact with the racquet—they just *know* when it is in the right place.

Human beings are very good at interacting with tools, and we learn to use them *intuitively*, in other words, in ways that work well with what the body does naturally. Whether it's baseball players, tennis players, or shooters, people can learn to use kinesthetic alignment with a high degree of precision that enables the hits they need.

In the context of defensive shooting, the distance at which most people will have to get hits is nine to 15 feet. Certainly, that distance is very likely, if you are limited to defending yourself inside your home. Just about all the students I've trained over the years are able to efficiently use kinesthetic alignment, along with all the other intuitive fundamentals of shooting, to place multiple rounds

The semi-crouched position as these shooters are demonstrating, is one natural to you when you are startled. You will automatically bend at the knees, lower your center of gravity, close down at the hips, and lean forward. The biggest benefit to such a position when you are armed to defend yourself, is that this very natural position also provides the most stable shooting platform.

quickly into the high center of an appropriately positioned chest-sized target at that distance. The ones who have not been able to have had significant physical issues hampering them, such as extremely debilitating arthritis, tremors, and/or strength issues (muscle deterioration in the elderly). Healthy people have no problem with this skill.

Some people immediately cry foul when they hear things like this and suggest that it's reckless to teach people to shoot without their sights. I will tell you that there are countless examples of people successfully defending themselves with no recollection of ever looking at their sights, and just as many documented examples of people being able to reliably hit chest-sized targets in the high center zone at comparable distances. Since there is overwhelming supportive data to prove this, I would say it is reckless *not* to teach people to shoot using kinesthetic alignment under appropriate circumstances. I think it is a great disservice to create a behavioral and mechanical dependence on sighted fire for all counter-ambush defensive shooting situations.

Kinesthetic alignment is an important part of the physics of defensive shooting. So is sighted fire. I do *not* want to insinuate that sighted fire isn't important. There's a time and a place for sighted fire, but you want your sighted fire to be intuitive, as well. That means starting with a solid foundation of placing the gun where it needs to be, simply by feel, then learning to refine your shot control, and then *increasing* potential precision by adding the use of the sights. As an aside, there is a common misconception out

there that people should train only in one or the other of either sighted or unsighted fire, and that is *far* from the truth. In the CFS Program, we teach sighted fire within an hour of the first shot going downrange and as we add targets that are often too challenging for most students to hit with kinesthetic alignment alone.

Notch and blade-type sights are indeed what you want on your defensive firearm. With them, you want to make sure you are able to align the blade of the front sight inside of the notch of the rear site with equal amounts of light on either side of the blade and with the tops of the front and rear sights level relative to the firearm itself. That is the most efficient way to control your shots at a high level with a defensive handgun.

When using your sights, your focus should be sharply on your front sight blade. To facilitate a *clear* sight picture, you should close an eye, because light travels in a straight line and our eyes are offset. Efficient, two-eyes-open sighted fire is another myth created by those who try to teach people to use their sights on chest-sized targets at close ranges. In fact, I used to teach it! In a training environment, you can perform two-eyes-open sighted fire somewhat easily, especially at targets for which you wouldn't actually *need* your sights (an eight-inch circle at 10 feet, for example). The relationship between the sight and the target you are actually trying to hit is pretty easy to figure out when the conditions are optimal, the target and yourself are completely static, and your brain isn't racing to figure out which of two target images (the double image that is often unresolved when using both eyes open), is the actual threat. So,

When it comes to sights on a defensive handgun, you should look for a wide rear notch and a bright, relatively wide, front blade. (Ameriglo® Claw EMS Sights pictured.)

in situations where you actually do need your sights, it makes much more sense to close an eye and acquire the sight picture more easily.

Sights are on your firearm to increase *precision*, not *speed*. All the sight designs that deviate from the traditional notch and blade merely increase your ability to be fast in times of relatively low precision requirements. That said, it is a good idea to augment your front sight with reflective paint or a bright dot, in order to make it more distinguishable. Adding similar markings to your rear sight to aid in a quick alignment may be good in some circumstances where you feel your sights are needed, but the precision requirement in such instances will still be relatively low. Personally, I prefer a wider than normal rear notch (.165-inch or .18-inch) and a standard width front sight (.125-inch). I find that this combination, with a bright front sight, is the best for defensive shooting situations for the overwhelming majority of people. (I developed the I.C.E. Claw EMS rear sight for defensive handguns as a very simple solution for my

students looking for an affordable option on their modern defensive pistol.)

THE HIGH COMPRESSED READY POSITION

So far, what I've mostly been talking about are the elements that provide a solid foundation for connecting your shot with the target. Let's expand on that and discuss some techniques that will benefit you in the event of an armed home-defense situation.

In the search for consistency and efficiency in every area of weapons handling and defensive pistol use, what instructors teach in regard to the "ready" position is one of the most troublesome areas. A ready position is the position you keep your gun when you are holding it, but not shooting. It should also be the position in which you place the gun when you are reloading it and clearing malfunctions—basically whenever you are holding it, but not actively using it to engage a threat.

I teach the ready position as a "High Compressed Ready" position. While there are certain positions that offer isolated benefits in extreme circumstances, what I teach in Combat Focus® Shooting is about addressing the most common, critical incident problems for the largest number of people. In pointing out the strengths of the High Compressed Ready position, the shortfalls of other positions will be more clearly evident. That is not to say these other positions don't have their own advantages in specific and individual cases, but I don't believe that any other position is as universally beneficial as the High Compressed Ready. The discussion here will center on how it works with a handgun (Chapter 21 will cover its use with long guns).

The High Compressed Ready Position is one that brings the gun in close to the chest, with the muzzle oriented below the line of sight, the elbows tucked at the shooter's side, and the shoulders, hips, and feet oriented towards the front. From this position, the shooter can easily reload, clear a malfunction, assess their environment, present the weapon towards the threat, protect the weapon from being grabbed, move it into an extreme close-quarters shooting position, or do just about anything else one might need to do during a dynamic critical incident, all with the most consistency and strength.

Let's break down some of these elements.

"Close to the chest" means, very specifically, your chest, not your belly. This is the "high" part of the High Compressed Ready. By keeping the gun up high in front of the body, you maintain more strength (arms bent, rather than extended), and control (it is harder for someone to reach the gun, when it is tucked against the chest). As you will see in the next section, it is also easier to present the gun consistently and efficiently, if the gun is held high in front of the body in this manner.

Keeping the gun close to your chest keeps the gun out of your field of vision. This allows you to assess the environment

The High Compressed Ready Position can be modified to a one-handed position, if you need to use your other hand to use a phone, a light, or open a door.

around you more easily, including anyone lying on the ground in front of you, and also the ground itself, as you move through a critical incident.

Keep in mind that the two-handed High Compressed Ready position I'm describing here is congruent with the idea that the fundamental two-day Combat Focus® Shooting course I teach deals exclusively with events that involve threats beyond two arms reach. If you find yourself in a situation with a threat that is within that distance, it is more reasonable to take your weak hand off the pistol and partially extend it to shield the pistol from any attempt to grab or reorient it.

Keeping the "muzzle down" is, at some levels, a safety issue. In training, as noted above, this is a very real concern. Luckily for us, it also makes a great deal of sense both tactically and when considering an economy of motion. The worst-case scenario for needing to use a handgun when we have it with us is that it is in the holster when we recognize the threat. In almost every case, that means the muzzle will be pointed down. In most recommended carry positions, the handgun will be coming through the area of the High Compressed Ready before it is presented towards the target. As the firearm reaches that point, the muzzle will either be pointed straight out towards the threat or be rotating into a position that orients the muzzle in that direction. Having the muzzle pointed up in the ready position means that your presentation from the ready position and the presentation from the holster would be inconsistent—and inconsistency is bad.

Next along the topic of muzzle down, consider any weapons handling function in which you might want to engage while you have the gun in the ready position. I recommend manually manipulating the slide by reaching the weak hand over the slide and behind the ejection port, whenever it's necessary to get the gun into or out of battery. Doing this with the muzzle pointed up is much harder and usually requires the gun to be pushed out from the body, resulting in more inconsistency when it comes time to present the weapon towards the threat.

The last major endorsement of the muzzle down position comes in the area of retention and extreme close-quarters shooting. If someone catches you off-guard and grabs your firearm with the muzzle oriented in an upward position, you will have to rely on your strength and technique to orient the gun back into a position from which you could use it against the threat. If the muzzle is oriented down, it is much more likely to be oriented towards some part of the threat's body, regardless their relative strength.

By keeping your "elbows tucked into your side," you create more of a barrier against an attempt to grab your gun from outside your field of vision. Think back to how I've talked about what your body does naturally. One of those natural things that happen to you during a dynamic critical incident is that your field of vision will be diminished. A physical barrier to someone grabbing your gun can help counteract this decrease in your peripheral visual acuity. You may also recall that one of the ways your body gathers information about an attack is through touch—consider your elbows and upper arms to be like a cat's whiskers, telling your brain about an attack before you can see it coming.

When using kinesthetic alignment, the gun will be placed directly in your line of sight, with both eyes focused on the threat.

Should that attack be against your torso and not a gun grab (for instance, a knife thrust), having your arms close in to your sides will also protect the ribs and abdomen much more than other ready positions. Too, with your elbows in this position, you should be assured of being consistently able to extend the gun out into a shooting position, instead of risking the swinging up of the gun from a straight arm ready position.

Last, keeping your elbows and arms tight into your sides produces very little fatigue, as you can actually be taking up some of the weight of the gun through your forearms on your midsection, body armor, or other gear.

By keeping everything oriented toward the front along your field of vision, you will be able to respond efficiently to threats visually identified. You are also less likely to have someone grab your gun from outside this field of vision or to bump your gun into something while you move or present it towards a threat. Bladed positions relative to your expected threat angle inevitably expose the firearm needlessly to attack from other angles, result in the necessity of repositioning yourself to respond to threats to the weak side, or have you swinging the gun towards a target that was identified laterally.

PRESENTATION FROM THE READY POSITION

The presentation of the firearm towards the threat is one of the most often flawed parts of an experienced shooter's program. In our buzzword-filled industry, many people mean many different things when they say "ready position." One

reason I teach and prefer the use of High Compressed Ready is because it's very easy to efficiently get the pistol into a shooting position from this specific position. But High Compressed Ready is also consistent with the movement of the gun out of the holster and into a proper shooting position. As I cover this, I'll focus on efficiency and consistency to guide the choice of technique in the presentation. That will lead us to economy of motion, a core concept of all of our mechanical skills.

How do you get the gun into a firing position as fast as you can? You want to get the gun into a position that *is in and parallel with our line of sight*. You also want both your arms to be at full extension (assuming a two-handed grip).

When the gun comes out of the holster to the High Compressed Ready position, the muzzle is aimed at a point that's lower than our line of sight to the target. Given that fact, we know that if the muzzle ever points *above* our line of sight, it is because of *extraneous* motion.

Let's step back for a moment and examine the way the brain controls our muscles. The actual presentation of the firearm from either the holster or the ready position is the single biggest movement that's going to be performed during the shooting portion of most critical incidents. With this in mind, it should be clear that you need to keep that presentation as efficient as possible. For this reason, and several others, you are going to want to extend our arms all the way out during the presentation. Why? If your brain has to start *and* stop the movement of the gun, you are doubling the mental effort in this part of the process. By sending one message—"Out!"—your brain is less cluttered than it would be if you were doing two different things with your arms, or if you were trying to arrive at an arbitrary position between having your arms against your body and having them fully extended.

It is very important, at this point, to understand what is meant by "in and parallel with the line of sight." If you picture a firearm pointed towards a target in front of a shooter but held at your hip, it is entirely possible to get the firearm parallel with your line of sight, but it is clearly not in the line of sight when it's at your hip. Similarly, if the gun is in your line of sight but canted offline, it isn't going to be consistently aligned properly with the target.

It is simple enough to get the gun in the right position eventually, but you must get it there as *efficiently* as possible. Think for a moment about the way the human shoulders and arms are built and move. If you fully extend the gun out in front of you but at an angle towards the ground and *then* rotate the gun into the proper position from the shoulder, your brain needs to send a message to the muscles to stop the movement as your arms reach the right spot. In such a case, you'll need to rely on muscle control to stop the upward momentum of the gun. Obviously, this is not an efficient way to get the firearm into the proper shooting position. It is a much better idea to use the way your body is built to stop the gun's movement for you. This means that you need to get the gun in and parallel with your line of sight *before* your arms fully are extended. By doing this, you ensure that the final movement of the gun will be out towards the target, where your arms will biomechanically lock automatically.

It should be noted here that, while your arms may not get to a point of being fully extended, extending as far as your range of motion allows while wearing heavy body armor or some other device or clothing across your chest will accomplish the same goal. "All the way out," is all the way out, regardless whether your arms are perfectly straight.

The real trick is to only move your arms in one direction at the end the presentation. That one direction is out towards the threat. If the final movement of the gun is a swinging motion—either up or to the side—instead of an outward movement towards the threat and eventually to a biomechanical stopping point, there will be momentum that must be stopped with muscular action. Inertia is the propensity of a body in motion (the gun in your hand) to remain in motion until acted upon by an opposing force. Inertia creates deviation, which means you'll have to slow down your response for more precise shooting by swinging your gun into position, as opposed to extending it. As Colonel Rex Applegate notes in *Kill or Get Killed*, "It will be apparent that it is very difficult to swing your arm horizontally in a new direction and stop it in time to obtain the proper windage for accurate firing. This is especially true in combat. Ordinarily, two-thirds of the shots will be fired at the target either before the weapon reaches it or after it has passed across it and is on the other side. You can't make your arm stop in the same place twice ... ." The observations made by Colonel Applegate, a true pioneer in the field of dynamic defensive shooting, are consistent with all modern empirical evidence and the way the body works.

CHAPTER 20

DYNAMIC ACCURACY

You've learned to shoot on a practice range. But the regimen and mental discipline of producing one-hole groups isn't likely to help you much when trouble is barreling down on you like a runaway train.

How many rounds will it take from your gun to stop a lethal threat? Is it reasonable to expect a single round to stop a threat? What is your goal each time you press the trigger?

When I ask these questions in a room full of "gun people," they usually focus on the last one and I usually get agreement on either "hit the target" or "stop the threat."

Hitting the target is actually a pretty good answer, but, in reality, it is a *target shooting concept*. This may not be enough in a survival situation. If your target was wearing hard body armor and you were shooting a .22, you may achieve anything by hitting your target. Granted that's an extreme example, but you have to try to have as universally applicable a goal as possible each time you pull the trigger. We all know that many people have been struck by bullets and not shown any immediate response. If someone is shooting at you and it takes one full second for a bullet's impact to actually cause them to stop shooting at you, they could fire another three, four, or even five shots!

"Stop the threat" might also sound good as an answer to the question of shooting goals, but we know from previous sections in this book that this is not a reasonable expectation from a single bullet, especially a pistol bullet.

Now, think about how you answered the second question at the top of this section. I say the answer to that question, and a reasonable goal for any defensive shot, is something I call "dynamic accuracy." Dynamic accuracy is defined as any shot that significantly affects the target's

ability to present a lethal threat. A couple examples will help here.

Say a man with a knife kicks in your door and starts moving towards you from across the room, yelling, "I'm going to kill you!" You recognize the threat, move laterally while drawing your pistol, but, instead of completing a proper presentation, you angle the gun out of the holster, start to sweep up, and shoot early out of fear. The round goes into the threat's leg and he falls and drops the knife. Guess what? Your shot, which was textbook wrong in at least a couple ways, still meets the definition of dynamic accuracy.

Now, picture the same guy, but this time he's right next to you when he pulls out the knife, brings it immediately up towards your neck, and knocks you down, pinning you to the floor. You block the stab with your hands, but realize that he is stronger than you, as the knife continues to move towards your throat. As you continue to hamper the motion of the knife into your neck with your weak hand, you draw your pistol and feel the knife cutting slowly into you. At this point, that same shot in the leg may not significantly affect the target's ability to complete the driving of the knife into your throat. In fact, you may need to shoot the threat through the brain to get the action to stop in time.

These two examples are extremes, in terms of the need for precision, but they are the ones I use in class to demonstrate the idea of how we are really only interested in the end result of any particular shot. Even if a shot misses the threat, if it causes him to cower, drop his weapon, stop his assault, and otherwise give up, the shot must be deemed dynamically accurate, according to the definition. This is hard for some people to get their heads around. The idea that a hit can do nothing and a miss can achieve a goal may be counterintuitive to tactically minded gun owners, but they are facts.

In a training mode, you have to have some target area on the paper, mannequin, or steel you're shooting. Looking at the body of empirical evidence from real critical incidents, I can say that, most of the time, a shot to the high center chest will significantly affect the target's ability to present a lethal threat. In training, that means most of your shots should be directed towards the high center chest

not overemphasizing concepts that come from target shooting regimens and, therefore, prepare themselves to stop threats faster in a real incident.

How about the question of how many rounds should you shoot? In the real world, it is vitally important to be constantly assessing the results of your shots on the threat. Luckily, most dynamic critical incidents occur at close ranges, where the brain's natural instinct to focus on the threat doesn't have to be fought against and hits can be achieved efficiently using good kinesthetic fundamentals. So, if you take the time to understand the actual goal

Even if your shot misses, if it causes your threat to drop his weapon, cower, flee the scene, or otherwise give up, the shot must be deemed to be "dynamically accurate."

area, understanding that both any hit in this region is equal to any other, and the more hits you can get in this area in the shortest amount of time the better.

This brings up another important concept taught by many, and that is the desire to produce one small knot of holes touching one another in the center of a silhouette target. I'll tell you that doing so probably just means you were shooting too slowly. I'll also add that I think specialty targets (hostage situations, threats behind cover, etc.), and scenario training, all of which require high levels of precision, should be used sparingly, mostly to augment standard skill development. By understanding dynamic accuracy, most shooters will be able to shoot faster by

of each round you fire, it should then be clear that you need to be prepared to fire as many shots as it takes.

Putting that concept into a practical setting and training realistically to perform as such is incredibly important. When training, be sure to vary the number of rounds in your strings of fire. Don't get into a habit of shooting any specific number of rounds, or "double-taps." Picture a threat and its cessation, and let that be what determines the number of rounds in a particular string of fire. If every round you fire during a critical incident is combat accurate, you will stop your threat more efficiently and, therefore, they will have less opportunity to hurt you or someone you care about.

The target range is mandatory to your training. But don't let static targets and regimented drills be the be-all-end-all of how you perfect your self-defense skills. You must mix things up—shooting positions, the number of rounds you fire in a string, and more—if you expect to be as prepared as you can possibly be to deal with a real-life dynamic critical incident.

BALANCING SPEED AND PRECISION

Of all the fundamental concepts within the Combat Focus Shooting Program, understanding the balance of speed and precision is the most important to achieving maximum efficiency with a firearm. This concept also helps to answer the ubiquitous sighted or unsighted question. The balance of speed and precision might be the most important thing a shooter should understand about training for the tactical use of a pistol.

First, a word problem. If you are hitting a given target 90 percent of the time at 10 feet and you move back to 30 feet, what percentage of the time should you hit the target?

I ask this question to most of my shooting classes. I let the question hang for about 10 to 20 seconds, while the students offer their responses. The most frequent responses are numbers between 60 and 80 percent. Almost always, someone will eventually say "Ninety percent," and, occasionally, someone will offer the notion of 100 percent as an option.

Ultimately, the last answer is the correct one. If you pull the trigger, you should hit your target. As a practical exercise, however, the point of the question is that your ability to hit a given target should be consistent within reasonable parameters, regardless the distance to the target. For the more nit-picky readers, 100-yard shooting with a pistol is not considered "reasonable parameters," but from five feet to 50 feet, the differences in hit percentage for a given shooter of any skill level should be minimal. What *is* going to change is the amount of time and effort any given shooter will have to apply to maintaining their hit percentage.

The fundamentals of the balancing speed and precision are:

- The target dictates the need for precision.
- The shooter's application of skill determines whether they get the hit (unless you get lucky).
- The shooter's comfort/confidence in their ability to get the hit determines the

The idea of combat accuracy is one that's a balance of speed and precision. Let loose of the bull's-eye mentality. If you're shooting knots of holes at defensive ranges of five to 50 feet, you're likely shooting too slowly.

speed with which the shot is taken (unless you are out of control).

If your training is realistic and frequent, the correlation between your confidence and your actual ability will be higher. Conversely, if you have only been target shooting and you do very well, you may be overconfident in your actual defensive shooting ability. The latter is typically the case, when an antiquated qualification system and training program leads a police officer to think of himself as a "90-percent shooter" and they then achieve less than a 50-percent hit rate during a real critical incident. Similarly, if you think you need to use the gun's sights to get combat accurate hits under all circumstances, you may be *under*-confident in your ability to shoot unsighted at a target only a few feet from you and, therefore, shoot more slowly than you could, thus extending the time you are in danger during a critical incident.

IN THE ZONE

One of the most significant changes in the focus of my program as it is taught today, as opposed to a few years ago, is on the overt stress placed on tying the execution of complex motor skills directly to the cognitive processing of information. The importance of this one aspect of firearms training is a direct result of the constant reexamination of the concept of the balance of speed and precision, as well as the drills we use on the range to develop a student's accurate confidence in their ability and understanding of how much shot control to apply in any given situation.

Too often, combative skill development has been favorably compared to athletic skill development. This philosophy has distracted us from most efficiently developing the ability to apply skills on demand (one of my program's primary fundamentals). Sports science has long known that high -level athletic performance is enhanced by visualization, isolated repetition, and being "in a zone." In the book *The Owners Manual for The Brain*, there is an out-standing description of how being in the zone, or finding what psychologist Mihaly Csikszentmihalyi calls "flow," assists peak performance, and even how having the proper flow can enhance skill development. Keys to being in this zone are concepts like concentration, focus, and visualization. Author Howard explains, "The individual is so absorbed in the event that nothing else intrudes into awareness."

What is often missing from our application of these sports-based concepts is what the definition of the word "event" might be in Howard's description. Certainly, thinking that we are talking about the entire dynamic critical incident as having our complete attention would be accurate. I do not, however, apply this level of attention to the specific action of shooting.

Unlike an athletic activity, such as a basketball free throw, the complex motor skills of shooting are not being performed in isolation, i.e., they are not being performed in a situation where "nothing else intrudes." In fact, many other things will be going on. I'll talk about this more in the chapter on the "Warrior Expert Theory," but here's something to draw on in the meantime:

The athletic ability to draw quickly and shoot straight is not nearly as important as the ability to recognize a threat as early as possible and respond appropriately and efficiently, utilizing the environment, training, and tools available to you.

Your shooting is going to need to be performed amid *myriad* distractions. Counter-ambush shooting during a dynamic critical incident is much more like a basketball player's on-the-move sky hook from the three-point line, under double coverage, at the buzzer, and for the championship, than it will ever be like a free throw! Of course, that shot is going to have a much lower percentage of success than the free throw, and that is why the third fundamental of the balance of speed and precision is so important: You must have an accurate confidence in your ability, if you are going to be shooting appropriately—as efficiently as possible, in order to stop the threat—under the conditions you find yourself needing to shoot. By tying the execution of the complex motor skills (shooting) to the cognitive processing of a stimulus, you are at least simulating the process that will occur on the street or in your home, if you must defend yourself with a gun; that's not likely to be a free throw situation, where you can visualize what you are about to do, focus intently, and then execute the skill.

If you think about *any* drill you've performed where you knew exactly what you were going to have to do after the command stimulus (buzzer, whistle, word), you were simulating a free throw.

If you have only one option after the buzzer goes off (a multiple-shot string to the high center chest, for example), you are able to visualize it, and your motor cortex will prime the *exact* set of neurons required to execute the skill. This is a huge advantage to the application of those skills that should not be underestimated. It is exactly why free throw percentages are higher than percentages of shots during the dynamic moments of a basketball game. Isolating the skill of shooting will result in higher performance, but that *artificially* higher level performance generated by such shooting routines can lead to an unrealistically high confidence in you ability to shoot or in the techniques that you have chosen. That inappropriately high level of confidence can translate into poor performance in an actual situation, because you did not apply the appropriate amount of control.

By engaging in drills that address a balance of speed and precision (described later in this book), you will learn to execute varieties of specific motor skills in response to varied stimuli. This simulates the conditions of defensive shooting much more accurately. Under real conditions, you will be responding to an unexpected set of stimuli that will dictate the need for precision and, therefore, the exact set of motor skills you will need. Per the Warrior Expert Theory, the more frequent and realistic your training is, the more likely you will be to recognize exactly what set of motor skills you need to perform adequately during a dynamic critical incident.

CHAPTER 21

BEYOND THE HANDGUN:

RIFLE AND SHOTGUN APPLICATIONS

Long guns can certainly have their place in a home-defense setup. Here's what you need to know before choosing one of these and its ammunition.

U p until now, I've focused exclusively on handguns for personal-defense in the home. But long guns can have there place, too. Let's explore some of those options.

DEFENSIVE RIFLES

If you are going to be in a static barricaded position, a home-defense rifle is probably the best tool you can have ready for the moment a threat comes through the last door or around the last corner. The primary advantage a rifle has over a pistol is that it is significantly easier for you to hit your threat with one. Other pluses include the fact that most rifles will offer increased power and capacity, and, with a rifle, you have four points of contact, instead of just the one you get with a pistol. Those four points of contact—control hand, support hand, torso and face—give you more feedback,

allow for more consistency in the rifle's position, and allow you to better control recoil during multiple shot strings of fire.

The types of rifles most people stage for home-defense will be semi-automatic and of medium caliber. Examples include the AR-15 and the AK-47 styles of rifles. These rifles can be set up for very efficient defensive use and employ detachable magazines that hold more than two-dozen rounds that are significantly more powerful than defensive handgun loads. The AK-47-type rifles are generally more reliable for the amount of money invested, but they are less ergonomic and less efficient to run.

In the civilian rifle classes I run, most people have AR-15-type rifles they train with for defensive use, and they are almost always chambered for the .223 or 5.56mm round. This is the same type of rifle I stage for my own personal-defense

use. As I write this, in 2013, you can expect to spend $1,200 to $1,500 for a model that's reliable, and another $300 to $500 on magazines, a sling, and some type of red dot scope that will further increase the efficiency of your control efforts. Add in $1,000 in ammunition and the cost of a training course, and having a modern semi-automatic rifle (MSAR) staged for home-defense, learning how to use it, and maintaining your skills can easily cost $3,000 to $5000 over the course of your first year of ownership.

Even if you go with the less expensive AK-47 option, you are still looking at a $2,000 minimum investment to be responsibly and reliably prepared with a typical MSAR.

Alternatives to the MSAR do exist that at least provide the increase in control that a rifle lends, if not also the power and capacity advantage. These rifles are not semi-automatic, but they can be fired very quickly at home-defense ranges. One of the most common rifles used in such a capacity is the lever-action

Long guns have some significant advantages, not the least among them a high capacity of powerful rounds in today's modern sporting rifles, like those most often seen in the AR-15 and AK-47 styles.

carbine. These repeating rifles have relatively short barrels, along with fixed magazine tubes that generally hold five to 10 rounds. For home-defense, they are most commonly chambered in pistol calibers or medium rifle calibers, though they can be found in .22LR, as well as some very powerful file chamberings.

Lever-actions are lightweight and relatively easy to use. They are also very inexpensive compared to MSARs and, so, should not be overlooked as an option, especially for those on tighter budgets. In fact, I've been known to have one of these rifles at the ready in vehicles and/or camping situations, and I have occasionally staged one for home-defense. The main disadvantage lever-actions have compared to MSARs isn't the speed with which they can be shot, as some may think, it is actually the time it takes to reload them, as they do not have detachable magazines. Also, malfunctions with lever-actions, though rare, tend to be harder to clear than those that happen in MSARs. In this light, they are sometimes seen as the "revolver" of the rifle world. You could

easily be set up with a reliable lever action, ammunition and training for under $1,200.

Another option that may fit some readers is a .22 Winchester Magnum rifle, especially when this round is in a reliable semi-automatic, as used to be offered by Ruger and as currently manufactured by Magnum Research. While the .22-caliber is not normally one we associate with personal-defense, there are some instructors who recognize it as a viable revolver round, but, generally, whenever you fire a bullet out of 16-inch barrel instead of a two- or four-inch barrel, you are going to get more energy from it, as the gasses have more time to push it through the barrel. This means that, if the round is viable out of a snub-nosed revolver where it has about the same energy as a .380 pistol round, it certainly must be considered viable when run out of a rifle barrel.

The AR-15 platform, now often referred to as the "modern semi-automatic rifle" or MSAR, is most often used as a home-defense tool when chambered in the .223/5.56mm round. While the guns and training to be proficient in them for a defensive situation can be expensive, the trade-off can be a powerful, ultra-high-capacity firearm.

Don't knock 'em 'til you try 'em. The lever-action rifle is one that has plenty of defensive "oomph," and its operation and size can be one a wide variety of people can handle well; and that's a consideration when members of your family are of varying size and age. Keep in mind that the biggest drawback to this type of firearm is that it's relatively slow and more complex to load, and also that, in calibers other than .22, capacity is somewhat limited.

Personally, I don't think that the .22 Magnum round offers any advantages from a revolver for a person capable of using a double-action revolver well. I *do* think that the multiple-shot string of fire speed and increased control it delivers out of a lightweight rifle for someone *not* capable of supporting an MSAR or running a lever-action well, make it a tool worth considering. Remember, rifles are easier to hit your target with than are handguns. If the choice for one of my family members is between a 9mm handgun they can't use as reliably or efficiently as a .22 Magnum rifle, I'm obviously going to suggest the latter. Hitting the threat is paramount.

DEFENSIVE SHOTGUNS

Another popular defensive firearm option is the shotgun. Defensive shotguns come in three basic varieties: pump, semi-automatic, and double-barrel. Before I get into the unique aspects of each, I want to cover features consistent with all shotguns and how they may or may not be a great choice for your home-defense.

As the name implies, these long guns are designed to fire "shot" instead of a single projectile. Shot comes in a variety of sizes, with target loads and birdshot being very small and buckshot being larger, and shot sizes can run all the way up to the same diameter as capable pistol rounds. Like a rifle, shotguns offer four points of contact, which means that they are easier to hit your target with than you can with a pistol, but they carry the same negative aspects as rifles do in extreme close quarters.

Shotgun bore size is measured in "gauge," rather than the caliber designa-

tion used with pistols and rifles. With shotguns, the smaller the gauge, the larger the bore, and, so, the larger the bore, the more powerful the rounds you fire will generally be. However, because of the great variety in loads available in shotguns, you could certainly find specific 20-gauge loads that are more powerful than specific 12-gauge loads.

In addition to the pellet size and powder load of each shell, length of shells can vary within gauges. In most cases, the longer the shell the more powerful the charge and the more pellets it holds. (In addition to the gauge, your shotgun barrel will tell you which length shells it can handle.)

These are just some of the things that makes shotguns a special niche in the firearms world; it's hard to generalize about them. To keep us focused on personal-defense uses, though, I've broken down the significant options when it comes to ammunition choices, so that you can think about which is right for you. Let's take a look.

1. TARGET LOADS/BIRDSHOT (SHOT SIZE NOs. 9, 8, AND 7): Birdshot is very light and, therefore, has very little ability to penetrate what it hits. Beyond a few feet from the muzzle, birdshot begins to spread out very rapidly and lose its energy. Birdshot is generally not recommended for defensive use, though it certainly has a couple unique advantages. First, most of the people who choose to load birdshot into their HDS do so because of concerns about "over-penetration," that is having their gun's shot, slug, or bullet go through the threat or through a wall, potentially posing a threat to someone else. Using birdshot dramatically reduces the possibility of this happening. There is no doubt that all the psychological effects of shooting at a threat will be present if you use birdshot and, at very close ranges, birdshot can deliver lethal wounds. Given the ranges likely to be encountered in home-defense, birdshot is a viable option, though not the *best* choice. Remember that your barricade plan should include considering the most likely angles of shooting and having you create reasonable backstops or clear paths to reduce the likelihood of over-penetration danger.

2. HEAVY BIRDSHOT (SHOT SIZE NOs. 6, 5, AND 4): These heavier birdshot loads

are going to give you more penetration into your threat than their lighter cousins. There will be fewer pellets for any given weight of load, but each pellet will have more momentum with which to push deeper. Otherwise, these rounds are very similar to the above. Naturally, as the pellets get larger and heavier, you increase the issue of posing a risk to someone beyond your threat or intermediate walls/doors. Note that, in this category of shot size, you will find very heavy and powerful Magnum turkey loads for both 12- and 20-gauge shotguns. These loads will generally offer dense patterns and higher velocities than loads with smaller, lighter birdshot, which translates to significant energy delivered to your threat at close range with still relatively light individual projectiles. If you choose to use birdshot, these are the types of shells I recommend.

3. SMALL-PELLET BUCKSHOT (SHOT SIZE NOs. 2, 3, AND 4): These are interme-

diate-momentum pellets for HDS consideration. There will be a relatively large number of pellets compared to the larger buckshot loads, which means you have a slightly greater margin for error regarding where on your target you hit (because the pattern will generally be wider, when all other variables are the same). Traditionally, No. 4 Buck has been a very popular recommendation for home-defense, but this entire family of loads distinguishes itself from the birdshot loads in that I've found them to pose a much more significant level of danger of injury for people on the other side of a typical interior home wall.

Shotgun rounds lend themselves to the development of many specialty loads, such as this "buck-and-ball" load from Winchester.

4. LARGE-PELLET BUCKSHOT (SHOT SIZE NOs. 1, 0, 00, AND 000):
These are the most common types of shotgun hunting rounds for deer, hence the name, and they make excellent choices for defensive use in shotguns. The traditional loads of choice for law enforcement and military shotguns also fall into this group. "Double Ought" (00) buck is by far the most popular size, generally found as a nine-pellet count in a standard 12-gauge round. The power behind these pellets can vary greatly from load to load, ranging from low-recoil options to very high-powered magnum loads. These heavy buckshot pellets are generally the same diameter as small handgun rounds and, while lighter, pose very similar danger of injury to people on the other side of typical home interior walls. This is the section of shotgun ammunition where you will find the most specialty loads designed for defensive use.

5. SLUGS:
Slug loads, which are measured in the weight of the slug (most commonly one ounce of lead in a 12-gauge slug loading), are very powerful defensive firearm loads. In fact, these are often the most powerful individual rounds considered for home-defense or law enforcement patrol officer use.

At close range, slugs deliver more energy than most big-game hunting rifles. Slugs essentially turn your shotgun into a powerful, low-capacity, close-range rifle. Many people consider 12-gauge slugs too powerful for home-defense, because even slugs that hit your threat are very likely to push completely through and pose a danger to others behind. Recently, Winchester Ammunition addressed this problem by creating a pre-segmented slug specifically for home-defense, as part of its PDX1 Defender line of ammunition. (Winchester also offers a duplex load in its PDX1 Defender line, which is loaded with a slug and three buckshot pellets.) This solid slug is designed to expand and quickly break apart into three smaller, lighter segments having a large amount of surface area, though each segment will have much less momentum than the whole. Having had the opportunity to test this example many times in ballistic gelatin through my work with the company, I can tell you that this round performs as designed and there is very little likelihood it would over-penetrate a threat.

•••

While the 12-gauge is the most popular size for home-defense shotguns, I have become an advocate of considering a 20-gauge option, as well. Twenty-gauge shotguns are significantly lighter and are easier to shoot quickly than their larger cousins. With a 20-gauge, you can deliver much more energy to your attacker than you can with a handgun. The smallest bored shotguns, the .410-bores (this is actually a caliber and not a gauge), are even lighter and offer even less recoil, but are not usually considered viable options for home-defense.

If you decide on a gauge other than 12-gauge, you will find fewer options in ammunition specifically designed for defensive use, though I predict that the industry will offer more options, especially in 20-gauge, in the future.

While the 12-gauge is the most popular choice in a home-defense shotgun, the 20-gauge shouldn't be left off your list of considerations. They can be easier to handle for a wider variety of members in the home, and they can often accommodate faster shooting.

Just as people are realizing that modern ammunition makes the 9mm a better option than larger handgun calibers for defense, I believe that more and more people are seeing the potential benefits of the 20-gauge option.

In addition to bore size, shot, and gauge, the choke of your shotgun's barrel plays a role in your shotgun's effectiveness. Chokes change the interior diameter of the muzzle of the shotgun barrel, and this has an effect on the dispersion of pellets in a shot load. The tighter the choke, the tighter the pattern. It is important to note that, at bedroom distances, all patterns will be relatively tight. Only the most open bore (a constriction known as "Cylinder") paired with the shortest barrel (generally 18 inches) and the smallest pellet loads will commonly result in patterns much bigger than a human torso at typical home-defense distances. Traditionally, a medium choke (in this range, a constriction choice of "Modified" or "Improved Cylinder"), has been used for home-defense. The most important thing to know, when you are deciding which combination to go with for your HDS, is that it is usually relatively inexpensive to change chokes (or even to change barrels to one with

a different choke), if you find your pattern at expected home-defense shooting distances tighter or looser than you want; the majority of modern shotguns are now equipped with screw-in choke tubes, which allow for speedy swap out. The common options, from least restriction to tightest are Cylinder, Improved Cylinder, Modified, Improved Modified, and Full.

After choke, shot, and gauge, your biggest decision when choosing a home-defense shotgun is which type of action is right for you. There are three options:

1. PUMP-ACTION: Pump shotguns are very much like lever-action rifles, in that they require a manual action to be performed between each shot. On the shotgun, that action involves moving the fore-end back towards the shooter to eject the just-fired shell and then back forward towards the muzzle to chamber the next shell. Like the working of a lever-action, this is a skill that can be performed very quickly, with practice. Also like the lever-action rifle, pump shotguns hold their ammunition in a tube under the barrel, those tubes generally holding three to nine shotshells.

Pump shotguns are considered very reliable, though the fore-end must be run vigorously and completely through its range of motion in order for the gun to properly eject an empty hull and then successfully and fully chamber a new live round. On the upside, pump shotguns can run any type of shell that will fit the individual model, from the lightest loads to the heaviest. On the downside, pump shotguns deliver a lot of recoil energy to the shooter, compared to that of a semi-automatic shotgun, because none of the energy is absorbed by the operation of the firearm itself.

Pump-actions are the most common type of HDS. Beware, though, of the myth that the noise made by racking the pump of a shotgun is likely to scare a home intruder away—and I would suggest that you *never* follow the advice once given by Vice President Joe Biden to fire a load of shotgun pellets into the air to scare away an attacker. Not only should you never count on a firearm to scare someone away merely by its presence alone, firing rounds into the air *could kill someone* in the area where the pellets eventually land.

2. SEMI-AUTOMATIC SHOTGUNS: Like

handguns and rifles of this type, semi-automatic shotguns require nothing more than the resetting and pressing of the trigger in order to fire multiple shots. Semi-automatic shotguns are generally less reliable than the average semi-automatic home-defense rifle, because they can be very sensitive to ammunition selection. Unless the right combination of power and shot charge weight is being used, semi-automatic shotguns may not cycle reliably. Some shotguns, due to the nature of their operating system, further

require the shooter's gun handling to be very stable, in order for those guns to run correctly, and that's something that may not always be the case in a defensive shooting situation. I advise you to be sure to extensively test the specific load you want to use with this type of shotgun, and though semi-autos have become more and more reliable over time, they are not my first recommendation for an HDS.

3. DOUBLE-BARRELED SHOTGUNS: While

some may consider the double-barreled shotgun a relic of a bygone era, I think it deserves to be considered as an HDS. While it clearly suffers in the area of capacity (two shells between reloads, one per barrel), the shells you do load are gong to be very powerful, easy to direct towards your threat, and capable of being fired very quickly from an extremely reliable firearm. There's a lot to be said for those advantages.

Double-barreled shotguns can be had in either side-by-side or over-under configurations. I don't believe either makes much difference, when it comes to home-defense purposes. Some double-barreled shotguns will have two triggers, one for each barrel, while others have a single trigger than operates both barrels sequentially on successive pulls. I prefer the latter type, for simplicity of operation. Due to a resurgence in popularity, which in turn is due in no small part to the success of Cowboy Action shooting competitions, some manufacturers are now offering double-barreled shotguns specifically for home-defense. As these competitors have demonstrated, with practice, one can learn to reload a double-barreled shotgun very quickly.

Regardless which home-defense long gun you chose, they all require specific training and techniques to be used properly. Clearly, while your tactics for a barricaded position don't really change, how you handle and position yourself and your rifle or shotgun in those locations will be slightly different than they will be with a handgun. Where you really need extra training and practice is when you're moving through your home with a long gun; because of the space needed to deploy them efficiently, the possibility of your threat affecting your movements with a long gun is higher than it is when you're carrying a handgun. Consider your scenarios carefully when adding a long gun to your defensive plan and practice accordingly.

LONG GUN HANDLING

While your tactics for barricade situations don't change at all, you will be in more danger of having someone interfere with your defensive plans if you are moving through your house with a rifle or shotgun. It is much easier for a threat to interfere with your ability to affect them with a long gun if they get their hand or hands on it than it is for them to do the same with a handgun—and it is much harder for them to get their hands on your handgun in the first place, by virtue of its small size and comparative short length. For this reason, and despite some of their benefits (and as I covered in the section on moving through your house while armed), a long gun may not be your best choice for a defensive firearm in a moving situation.

When you consider the ready position for a shotgun or rifle, I'll stress to you the importance of keeping the muzzle low. As covered in the section on extreme close-quarters situations, having the muzzle pointed up and raised high gives a threat an opportunity to get between you and the muzzle much more easily. Also, in order to get the muzzle pointed up, you need to remove the stock from your chest, which means it takes much more time to get the long gun back into a shooting position. For these reasons, it is better to progress with the muzzle pointed low and away from you.

I refer to the low muzzle ready position as a High Compressed Ready position, for a few reasons. First, it allows you to use the same terminology as you do with your handgun, which reminds you of the importance of consistency. The way I explain it is that the *stock is high* on the body and the *muzzle is compressed* in close to your legs. In this position, you have three of your four points of contact exactly the same as they are in your shooting position (control hand, support hand, and the toe of the stock pressed against your chest exactly where it will be when you are shooting). You get into a shooting position simply by raising the gun up to your cheek. The muzzle being held close to the legs means that it is less likely you will be telegraphing your position beyond a corner you can't see around. It also ensures you will bring the rifle up to your cheek and set a good consistent shooting position, when you need to shoot. If you leave the rifle raised when you aren't shooting, you run the risk of changing your cheek weld on the stock as you rotate towards a target and swing the gun laterally.

Again, as it is with the handgun, you can perform all your gun handling skills in the High Compressed Ready position. During training, if you find yourself getting fatigued while holding the gun in this position with one hand during reloads and/or malfunction clearing practice, you could slip the stock off your body and down under your strong-side arm. While this compromises the position of the stock, it is still much more consistent with the shooting position and faster to recover from than is a traditional high muzzle ready position.

CHAPTER 22

BEEFING UP THE FORT:

STRENGTHENING YOUR HOME AGAINST INVASION

Despite the message of a certain credit card ad, you don't need a moat of crocodiles around the perimeter, nor should you booby-trap your entrances with overhead buckets of hot tar, in order to protect yourself and home. There are much simpler (and smarter) ways of keeping out the bad guys.

You want to have not only a good exterior entryway, but also a good interior barricade. Strengthening your home against home invasion is an important part of your preparation. Just being ready to fight isn't enough. Try to avoid the fight, or at least delay it as long as possible.

Protecting your family starts with strengthening your structural home against invasion. Having real barricades, having real physical security is a must, if you take home-defense seriously.

A reinforced entryway is a great place to start in your efforts toward making your home a harder target to hit. The first thing a potential attacker should see when he approaches your house is a gate or a gated storm door. More than just a fence or simple screen door, there should be something present that locks and tells any potential intruder that you take your security seriously.

This may be all you need to keep your home and family safe. In reality, few criminals are violent, thrill-seeking predators looking for a fight or a challenge. Most are looking to steal easy pickings or prey on easy victims. If your home sends a message that you care and that you are trying, that you are not going to be an easy target, you will most likely get passed up by the professional predator.

Being safer doesn't have to mean that you are locked in a cave! While you may not have a fence or even a yard at all, if you have the budget, there is one simple security option that any home should be able to accept: a security-style gated storm door on the entryways. These gates are actually a storm door, a screen door, and part of the security of the home. You

You get what you pay for when it comes to deadbolts, so consider investing in the best you can afford. You also may need to consider strengthening the door's frame, perhaps upgrading the door itself to a stronger model with stronger strike plates, and using longer mounting screws.

can still leave these doors open during the summer and get the breeze and the fresh air, but because it is actually a reinforced steel door with a reinforced frame and a solid lock, you can be much safer than you would be with a traditional (and flimsy) screen door. The heavy-duty storm door tells an intruder that, if they do decide to try to get into this target, they're going to have to fight their way through.

When it comes to the entry of your home, your main entryway door is your real (and literal!) gatekeeper. It is what is going to keep you separated from everyone who's outside and keep your family safe (even for a short while). Again, it also sends a message to everybody on the

Reinforced exterior security storm doors should be a no-brainer. Also, note the peephole in the solid, glassless door (the stairwell you see is a reflection of this apartment's exterior), behind the barred exterior door. Very smart.

outside that you take your security seriously. The door should be solid, without large panes of glass, if any at all. You also want to make sure that you do not have large glass panels adjacent to your door, as that means not only is door frame likely to be weak, but also that criminals will have the option of simply breaking that side-panel glass to gain entry to your home. The entry door itself simply must be of solid material, either wood, fiberglass, or metal. Your door's frame should also be strong and your hinges mounted with upgraded screws.

Of course, your lock system and the way it integrates with the frame is a big part of your door's overall security. Obviously, you want to make sure that you have a deadbolt.

Deadbolts come in many qualities and styles and there is some solid truth to the admonition of "You get what you pay for." If you head down to the local big-box store and buy a deadbolt for $20, it is going to be better than nothing, but maybe not much. You can spend up to $200 on a high-quality deadbolt lock that has a hardened cylinder that resists defeat through drilling. The investment may be worth it, but you need to remember that the deadbolt is just part of your entryway's overall integrity. In every test of forcible entry, deadbolts of any quality can be defeated if they are combined in the door with today's typical weak strike plates, weak frames, and/or weak and shallow screws. Upgrading to longer, stronger mounting screws and a strike box on the frame side of the door will dramatically enhance the security of your entryway. With or without a strike box, you want to make sure that the throw of the deadbolt extends at least one inch out of the door itself.

Another thing that you want as part of your exterior door is some type of peephole. You want to be able to look through your (hopefully) solid door and identify who is standing on your porch. That's obviously not for a time when someone's banging on the door saying they want to kill you. If you've identified the fact that there's a threat outside your home who means you and your family harm, you're not going to go over to the door and look at them through the peephole. Evade, barricade, and get prepared.

Now, take away the known and imminent threat. If someone rings the doorbell, you are going to want to identify them before you open the door. Just because they were polite doesn't mean they're not a threat. When someone knocks at your door or rings that doorbell, you don't want to just walk up to that door and start unlocking and opening up your house. A peephole allows you to see exactly who is outside, so that you can make sure it's someone you want to allow through the barricades you've made the time, effort, and investment to put in place.

An alternative to the in-door peephole is to have a relatively inexpensive security camera mounted on your porch that allows you to view what's outside from inside your home and away from the doorway (usually via a computer or tablet feed), in order to minimize your exposure to potential harm if someone is planning on forcing their way through the door. Keep in mind, if someone's been knocking and you don't see them when you look out through your peephole (or on your camera feed monitor),

Security bars that brace a door against entry are a smart thing to have in your rooms designated as barricade points. They're also a great idea for travelers staying in hotels.

Back Yard Cam

Utilizing a camera system is a great way to see what's going on outside your home, especially near entryways, and without exposing yourself to danger.

ask them to step in front of the door. If they don't, you already know you have a threat on your hands.

The exterior door, the screen door, your door and deadbolt hardware, and the peephole all work together to keep people outside your home. But what if someone's already in your home and you need a place to barricade and keep yourself safe?

When it comes to an interior barricade, you want to be able to do more than just shut a normal, hollow-core, interior door. Typical bedroom doors without much hardware aren't really going to protect you, so create an interior barricade by swapping out your hollow-core door for a solid-core model and

install a keyed deadbolt of the kind you would normally put on an exterior door. You must use a solid door instead of a hollow one, so it can't just be punched or pushed through. Again, as with the exterior door, have a reinforced frame and other hardware, as well. Installing better doors and hardware on your home's interior rooms is easily a do-it-yourself job and one that can dramatically increase the value of your barricade area. If nothing else, such doors will at least delay the person who's trying to hurt you or your family, while you get your family behind you, make your 9-1-1 call, get your firearm in hand, and prepare for that worst-case scenario where you have to defend yourself.

CHAPTER 23

ADDED MEASURES:

SECURITY TOOLS THAT IMPROVE YOUR ODDS

Nope, still no crocodiles or hot tar, just some noteworthy "added armor" to improve the strength of your home's perimeter—and buy you some peace of mind.

Passive security measures are items that you purchase, install and/or activate in order to make your home safer, but without you having to take an active role in making them work. While money is the primary resource you will need to acquire these measures, some of them also require that you do employ them properly. It's kind of no different than if you buy a vehicle with four-wheel-drive capability, but you fail to activate the system while driving through snow and get stuck or slip off the road into a ditch. You'd feel pretty foolish, then, right? Now, imagine have a reinforced door that you forgot to close or a security alarm you neglected to set on the night your home was invaded by violent intruders.

In the security world, it is well known that all the massive measures in the world do no good if the human element doesn't do its part. As you read about these items and consider their value, remember that you will need to at least maintain them, if not actively ensure they are working and being used on a daily basis for them to do you any good.

ELECTRONIC SECURITY

When it comes to electronic home security, it is really amazing what can be done for a reasonable amount of money. For less than the cost of another defensive firearm, you can have a system with door sensors, motion sensors, cameras, multiple keypads, and the ability to contact both you and the authorities by cellular signal—and you can control it all from your phone!

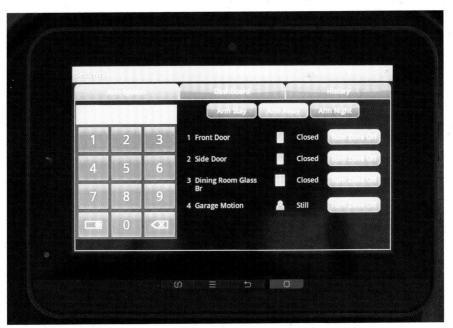

Alarm systems used to be a luxury, but today there are many affordable systems available. Just make sure you have access panels, with their emergency help buttons, in locations where you might need them, such as your barricade rooms, kitchen, etc., rather than just in your main entryway.

Used properly, today's electronic home security technology is so advanced, that much of the contemporary discussion about home-defense tactics shifts dramatically. Imagine you were awakened by a special ringtone from your phone that tells you your home's perimeter had just been breached. Then, with a swipe of your thumb across the touchscreen, you're shown a live video of a figure moving through your living room and towards the stairwell. How does that change your thought process and plan of action, compared to being awakened by the proverbial bump in the night? No, this book cannot be written with the assumption that you have this kind of technology at your disposal, but, in the future, it will be more and more accessible to those who want it.

DOGS

There is no doubt that one of the absolute best security investments you can make for your home and family is having a dog. A proper dog (not a miniature *anything*, not a dog that is happy to see anyone at any time, and not a breed that cannot survive without human intervention), can add more to your security than almost any inert tool or device. Dogs can serve as early warning systems, threat deterrence and, if trained properly, active physical defense.

There is a price to be paid for the four-legged asset. Dogs become a part of the family. Plus, of course, they need to be fed, cared for, and accommodated in the home. Not every home or living situation is conducive to having a canine as part of the security plan, but it should certainly be considered.

Chemical lights, just like the one your kids take to concerts or that you perhaps keep in your car emergency roadside kit, can be a great tactical tool when integrated into your home-defense plan. They can do the obvious, like illuminate the way in a pitch-black home, but wearing them or holding onto them and letting the police know you're doing so can help identify you and your family when help arrives.

LIGHT RESOURCES

While many people think they can cover lighting issues simply by staging a couple flashlights in certain areas within the house, or maybe even mounting one to their defensive firearm, there is a lot more to it than that! When you're fighting in the dark or, more importantly, you're trying to think about defending your home in the dark, you probably don't want to simply turn on a flashlight and either move to find your family or sit and wait for the bad guy.

As you move around a house with a light constantly on, it's very easy to predict your movement and know where you're going to be emerging through a doorway or around a corner—and that's exactly when you would get ambushed. Similarly, if you are sitting in a corner with a light shining on a doorway waiting for the threat, you are telegraphing your location and letting them decide when and how to strike your position. You really need to think about how you're going to use light inside your home.

I am not a fan of weapon-mounted lights. In fact, I am so much not a fan, that I lost out on the opportunity to be a columnist in one of the most popular gun magazines in the industry!

Many years ago, when handguns with rails on them were just starting to become the norm, I was checked out by an editor, as a precursor to being offered a somewhat prestigious column opportunity with him. Before I was formally given the spot, I was to write a few feature articles for the magazine. My first assignment was an overview on rail guns. I said to the editor, "Great! I've been wanting to talk about

The author is not a fan of lights mounted directly on your firearm. Keep in mind that everything you illuminate with such a light automatically has a gun pointed at it.

that. It's ridiculous to suggest to every gun owner that they should turn their gun into a flashlight or their flashlight into a gun!" The editor, who came from the hunting side of the industry and admitted he had no expertise with defensive firearms, was quiet for a moment. Then he bluntly told me that I needed to write a positive article about weapon-mounted lights. Apparently, there were a lot of advertisers who sold guns with rails and flashlights. I declined the opportunity to write the article and went on to focus my media energy on DVDs and TV. Chances are the editor and I are both happy with the way things worked out.

Despite the popularity of accessory rails, I still maintain the position that a person's primary flashlight in a defensive situation should be handheld. There is nothing wrong with having a secondary light mounted on your firearm just in case, but you need to keep in mind that everything you illuminate directly with a weapon-mounted light is naturally going to have a firearm pointed at it. I'd much rather you have a separate light in the hand that can be used intermittently and indirectly as you move through a house making sure family is secure or moving them to a barricade location. This means you are not going to shine the light directly where you're looking, nor are you going to leave it on constantly. While you could (and should) use a weapon-mounted light in the same way, you still end up using a lethal defensive tool for illumination—and that's a potential recipe for disaster.

I'm often asked why someone should use a flashlight intermittently and indirectly. The answer is because such activation of a flashlight will keep an intruder guessing, make it hard for a threat to figure out exactly where you are or where you are going at any given moment. You can use bounced light with a flashlight that's dedicated in your support hand, and then, if you need to use your firearm, you can either bring your hands together or simply drop your primary light and use a firearm-mounted light to illuminate your target.

Of course, most of the time, you're not going to be fighting in a pitch-black environment, but that doesn't mean some source of light in addition to natural ambient light can't help you. Chemical lights, for instance, are a great way to illuminate an area inside your home. In fact, using chemical lights, even when the electricity's off, is a great way to illuminate any environment you're going to be in. They also create a surreal environment inside your home that may psychologically affect an intruder; after all, who expects to see glowing green or orange chem sticks strewn about the inside of your home? Clearly, anyone using them has some type of plan and is prepared. Unless the intruder was already set on finding and hurting you, this tactic alone could cause them to reconsider their choice of target and retreat. You can also use chemical lights to indicate the room you want your family to go to, or maybe to indicate areas you've already surveyed, as well as set a path your family can follow to get to a barricaded area. You can use chemical lights to illuminate the area where the bad guy's going to be, which can cause him to be backlit, affecting his ability to see you in a dark area and/or assist in actually identifying

Darkness can be a huge advantage to you, during a home invasion. You know the layout of the home, where doorknobs and furniture are, and you certainly know where in the house you are—and the bad guy does not!

who is in your home. Of course the way you use those chemical lights should be part of your emergency plan, when you think about home-defense and discuss it with your family.

GOING DARK

At the end of the day, it might be that we worry about light way too much, when all we really need to do is turn the lights on. With the lights on inside your house, naturally you're going to be able to see everything you need to see. There will be less confusion and much less chance you'll mistake someone you know as being a threat. This alone may be worth any disadvantage to making the whole house bright as soon as you think someone is posing a threat.

On the other side of the equation, if you believe your home was secure and that all your family/home members are accounted for, sometimes darkness can be a huge advantage to you. Yes, darkness can be a disadvantage if you're someplace unfamiliar to you. But, if you're in your own home, being in complete darkness may be the best advantage you could possibly have, because the bad guy has *no* idea where you are—and he most likely doesn't know the layout of the home. He doesn't know the floor plan, the location of the furniture, or where the doorknobs

and light switches are. Such an intruder, and this would be most of them, will have a harder time finding and hurting you if they are confused in the dark.

Another thing you might think about? If the lights are going to be off, your family can use those chemical light sticks to illuminate and identify themselves. There are special chemical light packages available that come with small identification bracelets or necklaces that your family can put on in an emergency as part of your plan. They can be handed out ahead of time as part of your planning and practice, then kept in your family member's bedrooms or other private spaces for use as needed with an intrusion happening in a dark house.

There's yet another use for glow sticks. Say your kids are moving through the house, coming to the barricade area according to your plan, and they're clearly marked as non-threats as they come around corners and through doorways. Use this information to signal law enforcement. You can say to the 9-1-1 operator, "My family is wearing glow bracelets." They'll pass that intel onto the officers actually responding, and now those officers will know that anyone moving through the house with a glowing bracelet on their arm is probably a good guy.

CHAPTER 24

REACH FOR IT!
IMPROVISED HOME-DEFENSE TOOLS

Your best-laid plans have left you separated from your gun at the moment you least want to be. What's the next best thing to reach for?

W hen we talk about armed home-defense, we're generally assuming the use of a firearm to defend ourselves or families. But it's entirely possible that you may find yourself at home without your firearm on your person or that you may not be able to get to the firearm(s) staged for home-defense when you actually need it. Maybe you live in a jurisdiction or under circumstances where you can't have a loaded firearm ready, you can't have a firearm in a quick-access safe, and, in fact, your firearms must be and are secured in a vault that has much slower access. Maybe you have to keep your firearms and your ammunition stored separately. Maybe you've decided that firearms ownership isn't for you. Or, maybe, as is often the case, the threat

Kitchen knives should be an automatic go-to choice, when you find yourself attacked in your kitchen (or anywhere nearby) and without your firearm. But don't forget things like that wine bottle, which can be used to impact a threat, or even cut if you break the bottle.

you are up against inside your home is someone you previously trusted and didn't think you needed to protect yourself from. This last scenario is, unfortunately, very common for women who are sexual assault victims. The overwhelming majority of women who are assaulted in their own homes are victims of people they knew, not violent strangers who burst through the doors.

Of course if you're in one of those situations, it doesn't mean you're completely defenseless. It means that you're going to have to improvise a defensive tool. It is a great idea to think ahead about how you will defend yourself when you are without your gun, and the things in your environment that will help you.

In the kitchen, naturally, one of the first things you'll have at your disposal is a knife. Any type of knife will do, whether it's a big fillet knife, a steak knife, a butcher's knife, or a large carving blade. Any type of blade can be employed in ways similar to how you'd deploy that tactical folder or fixed blade you carry around or have trained with.

What other things might you find in a kitchen that can be used for personal defense? Maybe pans. Maybe you could take a pan and swing and hit someone. The edge of pan isn't sharp, but it's certainly something that's heavy and that you can use to impact someone with. If it's on the stove and you're actually cooking, don't forget that you would also have whatever hot contents are in the pan. Or the hot pan itself could be used, not just for blunt force, but to apply pressure and actually burn someone to get them to stop doing whatever it is they're doing. Of course, you could also launch the contents at someone to distract and *then* hit them with the empty pan.

You might find a glass bottle of some kind in the kitchen. Maybe you've got a bottle of cooking oil, wine, or other alcohol in the kitchen or somewhere in your home that could be heavy and used as an impact tool. You might even stage a bottle or two as a decoration that could be used for defense. The important thing is to start thinking ahead of time. Move through your house and look for things that could be used in a worst-case scenario.

As you move from the kitchen and into an entry area, now look to see if maybe you have a coat hanging in a hallway that could be used to smother,

The kitchen is ripe with self-defense objects. From sharp cutlery, heavy pots and pans (and even their hot contents), glassware and bottles that can be used as impromptu impact tools, and even your plates, platters, and cutting boards, all can help keep a predator at bay.

Yup, a mop may be what's closest at hand when a threat ensues. Keep cognizant of these types of objects in your home and their locations, so that you can automatically move to them if needed, especially when getting to your firearm isn't an immediate possibility.

blind, or at least hamper someone in their efforts to grab or hit you, even help defend yourself against a knife attack. Maybe you've got a mop or a broom somewhere leaning up behind a doorway or in a corner. You could certainly use something like that as a striking tool; although it's not very heavy, it would be very fast. More importantly, you could use it for pressure and distance, for pushing and holding someone back off of you. You could use this type of tool to block any impact or edged attack, too.

As you continue to move through the house, look for heavy objects. Maybe you've got some knickknacks on a shelf somewhere that could be used if they are very heavy. Maybe you've got books, big books, large, coffee table-type books that could be used not only to impact a treat but also to do something like block a knife attack. Lamps, too, can work, and decorative rocks are commonly seen on tables or shelves—but are they really decorations or are they impact tools staged for defense? I say, "Both!"

You might also have drinking glasses setting around your home. First and foremost, and just like a bottle, a drinking glass can be used as an impact device. If it broke (or if you broke it on purpose!), you'd get a sharp edge that you can use to cut or stab an attacker.

Another thing people don't often think about when it comes to home-defense are all the cords you have inside your homes. Cords can be used to entangle someone. Maybe you could even

use one to choke someone, if you had the opportunity to get it around their throat. You could control a hand, arm, or weapon with a cord, or you could even whip someone with the loose end of a cord to cause pain and distraction.

Inside a home office, you might have many things that you can use to defend yourself. The most obvious ones, like pens and pencils, can be stabbed into the eyes or throat of your attacker. Scissors can also be used to stab or employed as a blade, not exactly the kind of blade you have in a kitchen knife or a defensive folding blade, but one that's still a sharp, metal edge that can be used as a defensive blade to either pierce or slash.

Think about the chair that's in your office or dining room. You could pick it up ad use it to strike someone. You could also block and maintain your space outside your attacker's reach, as you move to a barricade, call for help, or obtain a better defensive tool.

•••

The point of this exercise isn't to purposefully stage weapons all around your house. The idea is to think about what things you could use if you needed to in the worst-case scenario, to help you defend yourself in your home when you don't have your firearm. This thought process will also prepare you to defend yourself effectively in someone else's home, a hotel, an office, or anyplace else you might be attacked and find yourself without your preferred defensive tool.

PART III

REALITY-BASED TRAINING

CHAPTER 25

THE WARRIOR EXPERT THEORY:

TRAINING FOR THE FIGHT

You practice twice a week at the indoor range, and you're a B-class IPSC competitor working on your A card. Think you're prepped, think you're well-trained for a down and dirty fight in your home? Think again ... .

In your training endeavors, you want to develop an automated relationship between a "learned stimulus" and a "learned response." Developing a learned response to things that happen around you is important, because intuitive responses can be improvised in the heat of the moment.

We have all seen or seen evidence of people who fail to execute their planned responses—ones they had practiced repeatedly in training—during actual incidents. It is frustrating for people to realize this has occurred in them, especially when they survive an incident for which they had heavily invested in prior training. Interestingly, until we entered the age of the ubiquitous security camera, most people either didn't know this was happening or they were in denial. In fact, it's taken more than a decade of reviewing video recordings of people defending themselves in real-life situations to get many to accept the fact that the traditional training models were failing (and face it, it isn't easy to hear that your hours of hard training didn't actually do you any good in your fight).

How does that *happen*?

YOU CAN'T OUT-TRAIN YOUR INSTINCTS

Generally, your training will fail you when you don't train to do intuitive things in an intuitive way. If you don't train for your planned learned response to be directly tied to the predicted action (the stimulus) to which it should respond, your brain may just jump to something else, when your instinc-

tive reactions kick in. Reactions, not responses, are *automatic*; they don't need to be practiced, though you might need to integrate them into your training, where appropriate.

"Instinctive" and "intuitive" can sometimes be confused. Instinctive reactions happen automatically as a result of stimuli. Reactions are not things you have to learn. Things like increased heart rate, focusing your eyes on a threat, and lowering your center of gravity when startled are all instinctive. You don't need to learn them, and you can't unlearn them in any practical way (and you really wouldn't want to anyway). Instinctive things are what your body does naturally.

Intuitive things *work well with* what your body does naturally. If something comes in as a stimulus that you're unfamiliar with and you don't have a stimulus response pattern that has been learned, all you can do is respond intuitively. Also, and perhaps more important to this discussion, if your learned response is completely incongruent with what the body does naturally, you will be *forced* to improvise. You will have to come up with *something*, and that thing your body comes up with is, by definition, going to have work well with what the body does naturally.

Unfortunately, something I've consistently seen over the years in the professional training world is people being taught things that do not work well with what the body does naturally. Many of the exercises, tactics, and techniques that have been taught and practiced in so-called "defensive shooting" courses have absolutely no con-

Many people say you will resort to your training in a real fight. This is simply not true. If you have trained in ways incongruent with the nature of actual defensive situations, your carefully honed skills may never come into play.

nection to learned stimuli or could be considered intuitive responses.

One good example of this is the classic Weaver shooting position. This often-taught shooting position starts with a bladed stance, the weak arm's elbow cocked down and the weak hand pulling back on an extended strong hand. You've probably seen this position in many TV police dramas or being used by target shooters at the range. This position works really well as a choreographed, mechanical platform, when shooting in a controlled environment (like a bull's-eye competition).

The biggest problem with this position is that, despite decades of people practicing it, I have *never* seen it actually performed in a real-life counter-ambush shooting situation; I have seen literally hundreds of actual, real-life shootings on dash camera and surveillance video, and I have yet to see this position used by any trained professional or amateur in response to a dynamic attack. I've never even seen it in the innumerable videos I've viewed of people in *simulated* ambush and firefight scenarios, and I've never seen anyone go to this position in a high level, reality based ambush scenario during training sessions I've run. In fact, I've never seen a single

law enforcement professional, military professional, novice, or anyone else, for that matter, *ever* use this position outside a controlled situation or as a secondary response after employing a much more natural position first. I have even challenged those who stand by teaching this shooting position to provide me with proof that anyone ever has. To date, I have yet to be provided with evidence that this counter-intuitive shooting position has any application whatsoever in *any* real-world scenario. Despite all this evidence (or lack thereof), several schools around the country continue to teach this outdated technique, doing a great disservice to those students who are serious about developing efficient defensive shooting skills.

A cliché I've heard used to refute my views on this issue is this: "You will default to your training in a real fight." I hate to be the bearer of bad news, but the empirical evidence says that *this is simply not true*. If you are training in ways that are complicated and incongruent with the nature of actual defensive situations, your carefully honed skills may never come in to play. If you are training in a way that doesn't integrate the body's natural reactions to being startled, you can't count on being able to magically apply your training into real-life, break-neck-paced action, when you are *actually* ambushed.

So, if we agree that it is unlikely your body's intuitive response to an ambush will be the same as many of the techniques used in controlled environments, let's examine the context in which your training *will* translate to a real-life scenario. Since intuitive actions work well with what the body already does naturally, the principle can be extended so that intuitive actions work well with the physics of a gun, and work well under bizarre or unexpected circumstances with other

Training to shoot around a barricade like this, which might just resemble having to defend yourself in your home's upstairs hallway, is better than standing squarely over a bench to shoot at a static target while you perfect your "perfect form." In fact, training like this can really help when you learn how your body naturally accommodates such obstacles. For instance, you learn how far you must angle out of the door opening to get the shot without exposing yourself too much, how you must balance your body in such a position, where your hands must be so that the slide operates fully and correctly, and other things that, again, naturally enable you to deal with real-life situations. In that light, the question becomes, if you don't know how and haven't trained to shoot out of a doorway and down a hallway while staying as concealed as possible, what will you do when you actually have to do that to defend your life? Will improvisation save your life?

variables that may exist in our dynamic critical incident.

THE POWER OF RECOGNITION

The limbic system is the part of the brain that seeks out the most efficient way to respond to any given situation. This is where recognized patterns are processed and planned responses are initiated. If there is no planned response tied to the pattern of information collected by your senses, you will *improvise* a solution.

It's not only in the absence of training, but also sometimes because of poor

training, that we see improvised responses. So, if you can develop intuitive, learned responses that work well with what the body does naturally, what you end up being able to do is use the power of the limbic system to access learned memories *and* send messages to your motor cortex and the rest of the body to respond as quickly as possible, regardless whatever cognitive distractions there are.

Trained, intuitive actions happen much faster than you can perform skills in a mechanical, choreographed, cognitive environment. What you're taking advantage of here is the power of *recognition*. Recognition is an incredibly powerful attribute. I talked about the power of recognition in my book on intuitive defensive shooting, *Combat Focus Shooting: Evolution 2010*. Recognition is the method of the expert. Expertise is developed through repeated exposure to information, patterns, and experiences over time.

People use recognition most commonly through the act of recognizing people. When you walk into a room and you recognize a person, you *know* that you know them. You may not be able to rattle off their entire resumé and family tree, but you know that you know them from *somewhere.*

We all know what it means to recognize someone in this way. Usually, people take this for granted, because they interact with the same people— family members, friends, coworkers, store clerks, restaurant staff, etc.—over and over again. Other times, the power of recognition seems absolutely amazing, such as when you see someone at an airport whom you haven't seen in years, or when you recognize someone you went to high school with 25 years ago, as you walk through the mall.

Recognition is incredibly powerful, so powerful, in fact, we sometimes even recognize a person based on circumstances. If you look out your window into your front yard and there's a guy wearing a uniform with a gun on his side, you probably aren't going to think, "Oh my gosh, a foreign army is invading!" You *recognize* that armed police officers do, in fact, exist in your town. You recognize that person intuitively by the circumstances and context in which they exist.

Now, let's approach this same idea from the perspective of instinct. Let's say you were just involved in a defensive shooting in your home. Immediately after the shooting you would, ideally, assess your environment. In that process, you may see someone approaching with a gun pointed at you. At that point, you *should* be startled—as should anyone! In this instance, however, the person approaching you with their gun drawn and pointed is wearing a uniform. *In that moment*, you know intellectually that there are police officers in your town, and your mind should be simultaneously going through an automatic recognition process.

Hopefully, you *recognize* that you need to surrender to the officer in that situation (after all, they're just doing their job and they may not realize you are the good guy). Obviously, the police officer is not someone you want to turn towards and shoot, even though they have a gun pointed at you. Instead, you recognize that you want to let them know you're a good guy, you're not a

Trained, intuitive actions happen much faster than you can perform skills in a mechanical, choreographed environment. What you're taking advantage of here is the power of recognition—and recognition is the method of the experts.

threat, that they don't need to shoot you, and that you're not going to shoot them.

Let's take on a different scenario. Let's say you're just having dinner and you're startled by a man who does not have a uniform on, who's kicking in your door and turning towards you and your family with a gun, and who has an angry facial expression and is yelling threats. Your recognition would be, should be, different. In this case, after your initial, startled response, you would *recognize* a threat and respond appropriately. In this light, it should be easy, now, to see how a separation between instinctive reactions and intuitive responses makes more sense in the context of recognition.

At I.C.E. Training Company, we teach a concept that relates to the way our brain uses intuitive responses. It relates about *how* we should train and, in some ways, *what* we should train. We call it the "Warrior Expert Theory." In this, experts learn to use the power of recognition to respond to patterns of information more efficiently.

If you were to walk up to the average patrol officer and ask them, "What's the code section for domestic violence in your jurisdiction?" or, "What's the code section for a DUI in your jurisdic-

tion?" you would probably get an instant recognition moment from them. If they are actively working a patrol shift in the U.S., unfortunate as it may be, those are two charges they're probably writing up regularly, so they should know exactly what one or both code sections are. Now, if you were to walk up to the average non-police person and ask them what the code section is for domestic abuse charge in the state of Illinois, you probably won't get an instant answer facilitated by recognition (yet, anyone with a smart phone and 35 seconds of free time should be able to use a search engine to find the answer for you). The point: Someone who is an *expert* recognizes information, while everyone else has to figure it out.

So the idea of the Warrior Expert Theory is that, through frequent and realistic training, you can learn to use the power of recognition to respond more efficiently during a dynamic critical incident. Through frequent and realistic training, you can take advantage of the system your brain has developed for executing learned responses to learned stimuli through the power of recognition.

This is huge! It means you aren't going to have to go into a laborious analytical process before taking the most appropriate and efficient action. You can actually cut the cumbersome cognitive processing out of the loop, and we know from studying humans under stress in clinical environments that this is a good thing; the way the brain operates under extreme stress makes accurate analysis less likely and more difficult. Scientists confirm this, by studying animals in a clinical environment at a greater level of detail. They can actually put electrodes into their brains, witness how they're reacting, and see how their brain operates under stress and fear. We also gain insight by looking at how humans whose brains have been damaged (whether through illness, disease, or a traumatic accident) operate, react, and respond—we can see how powerful recognition can be in the worst-case scenarios.

CONSISTENCY

How does this relate to preparing for home-defense? If you store your only defensive firearm in six different places at six different times, you are less likely to be able to *recognize* what you need to do to get your gun into action in a worst-case scenario. As a result, you are going to be less efficient in a fight, less efficient because your lack of consistency will have meant less exposure to the procedure for recovering and drawing a gun from any one of those places. Even if you train frequently to retrieve the gun from a variety of locations, the consistency of your training will suffer and, thus, you will not be *realistically* training and preparing yourself for action.

Realism is enhanced by training in ways that are consistent with the way you may have to fight. The more variables you introduce and, therefore, have to cover in your training, the less trained you are in any one of those areas. For example, if you sometimes store a gun loaded in a quick-access safe in your bedroom and other times you place it unloaded in a drawer in your kitchen with a magazine next to it, you create confusion in your brain, when your dog starts barking and you hear someone screaming and kicking at your back door. If you equally divided 100 home-defense drills, you are only *half* as practiced as you could be at getting to your gun and becoming ready with it. This reduction in specific training repetitions also comes into play when you choose to use different types of firearms, holsters, or any other defensive tool or technique. Nothing inherently good comes from practicing two overlapping ways to reload your gun, for example.

This brings me to the failure of another typical training cliché: "Having more tools in your toolbox is better than fewer." That phrase has been used to justify the wasting of more time than any other lesson I can think of in the training world. What you should do is find the best tool and practice with it as much as you can. Don't dilute the expenditure of your valuable training resources with redundancy.

While you are limiting the things with which you need to train and the techniques you need to practice, you should be sure you're integrating everything you *do* need to. If you don't integrate the startled response, think about how your family may be involved in your home-defense plan, or neglect to store a firearm in a consistent way, you might not know where

While you should limit the things with which you need to train, as well as the techniques you practice, you still must be realistic. Keep your gun in different places or practice for situations that happen only at your front door, and you may find yourself in trouble.

your gun is or how to get it until you cognitively, deliberately think, *Oh yeah, I put my gun in the safe last Tuesday. I need to go downstairs to get to it.* That's going to cause you to delay.

On a practical level, the amount of time this thought process would take is incredibly small. You most likely wouldn't even have time to say those words to out loud, before your brain figured out what it needed to do and did it. However, regardless of the speed of thought, the process would still need to take place, because you wouldn't have *automatic recognition.* And why set yourself for *any* delay in a worst-case scenario? Counter-ambush training seeks to find as many advantages and shortcuts as possible.

Allow me to be even more extreme: Let's say I keep my gun in the same place, a quick-access safe in my bedroom, but I have never actually practiced getting it quickly. Instead, in my practice, I am always very calm and precise when I take my gun out. I also train from a lane bench/tray setup in an indoor target range, an environment where I just pick up the gun, load it, get into my shooting position, fire my group, unload my gun, put it in my bag, and go home and place it back in the safe. So what happens the next

day, when I'm startled by the sounds of my door being kicked in and my daughter screaming and running upstairs? I know I must respond, but I have never practiced *realistically* for this. So now I run to the room, and I'm standing at the safe. In that moment, my brain says, *Respond!* But I don't have any expertise in getting my gun out of my safe efficiently, because I haven't trained for it! Whatever happens next has to be improvised in the moment.

I've seen this in real-life law enforcement and security situations. I've seen guys struggling to execute relatively simple skills for which they never trained in context. They haven't practiced rapidly getting to their gun or getting the gun out and driving it out. They fumble, and their presentations are sloppy. When this sort of thing occurs, the person in question will often fire their first shot from out of position and miss with that first shot (and usually several subsequent shots). You can avoid these foibles by developing expertise and strong stimulus/response patterns.

Practice realistically obtaining your defensive firearm after recognizing a threat. Because of the nature of most training environments and programs, a lot of people who carry a firearm for self-defense never practice that incredibly important skill, let alone practice it frequently and realistically. If you don't practice it frequently and realistically, you can't develop expertise. If you can't develop expertise, you can't use recognition, which is the incredibly powerful method of the expert. When it comes to all your predictably needed skills, you want to train often and realistically enough to rely on recognition. That means that your training must be designed to develop recognition, so you don't rely on choreography or staging to elicit your responses.

Let's look at the example of reload training with a semi-automatic firearm. During your practice, you should mix your strings of fire so that the gun gets to slide lock at some point you weren't necessarily expecting. When you feel the slide lock (when you wanted to shoot another round), you're simulating the context of a fight. Face it, in a real fight, you don't load one round at a time—that's not how a fight goes! In a fight, many shots are fire and, if you fire enough, your gun's slide will lock back. You need to be able to recognize what that stimulus feels like. You need to be an expert in slide lock.

The difference between the slide going back and forth and the slide locking back is *significant*. When you feel that slide lock back, you don't have to think about it or be aware of it. You non-cognitively (based on a learned stimulus response pattern) pull the gun in, drop the mag, reach for a fresh mag, insert it, rotate, rack, and continue fighting. If at any point in that chain you have to *intentionally* think about how to hit the release button or where your spare magazines are, it could create a delay in your response time that becomes catastrophic. The Warrior Expert does not risk suffering that delay. You should always be striving to increase your warrior expertise so that you can use the power of recognition.

COMPETITION— MOSTLY, IT'S JUST A GAME

Many people obsess over timers and running supposedly important drills over and over again. Typically, these types of drills have a pattern of set shots, set targets, and often set actions, such as staged reloads, that must be performed. The most ubiquitous of these drills are dubbed "qualification courses." Traditional qualification courses are just drills during which you perform you skills in a very choreographed way and are measured by shot group size and time spent to achieve the group. This is a great way to measure isolated shooting skills. But if you only train to get good at the qualification course, you only get good at those isolated shooting skills. You, wanting to have a plan for armed home-defense, need to develop skills in context. A true evaluation, a true "qualification," should be looking at your ability to apply your skills in context, not just perform them.

Many people believe that shooting competitions can substitute for training. I do not agree. Shooting competitions inevitably involve predictable, choreographed patterns, so that each participant's score can be compared. Far too often, that results in people compromising their gear, techniques, and tactics in order to get a better score.

Many people in the shooting community take offense to those of us in the training world who do not hold timers and scores up on a pedestal. Many even take the position that we have somehow attacked competition shooting. This is unfortunate. Personally, I am all for shooting competitions when people participate for fun, and I admire the shooting abilities of those who are able to compete professionally. As long as people keep the game in perspective and understand that it's a sport (even one that may have some, though certainly not a complete, overlap with defensive shooting), I think a little competition might even be a good way to motivate defensive shooters to get out and shoot more often. But, at the end of the day, boxing is not a street fight.

When you go into a ring, touch gloves, and agree to fight by a set of rules, you start to trust those rules and count on the controls you know are in place. In competition shooting, the number of variables is immeasurably smaller than in a real fight. The amount of stress, the type of gear, the number of shots and the potential angles and positions in a real fight for your life are all so far beyond what can be safely and fairly integrated into a competition environment, that it should be obvious why that forum is limited in its value as a training venue. The most important differences between qualification courses or competitions and the actual counter-ambush moment in a live fight is that the former two produce no need for you to recognize that you are suddenly in a fight, nor do they demand you process

information and apply your skills under unexpected and extreme stress.

It is important to note that you shouldn't obsess over objective standards in your training. Objective standards are incredibly important in administrative, bureaucratic, and competition environments. If you need to "qualify" to carry a gun or earn a spot on a special team, yes, you'll need a score. But, in a pure training environment, I am of the opinion that objective standards can get in the way of people reaching their maximum potential and/or staying true to their training goals.

Many people enjoy putting scores into their training regimen. No doubt, scores can be motivating. Unfortunately, they can be so motivating that people begin to obsess over their score in a controlled environment and focus less on developing their intuitive skills to as high a level as possible. Inevitably, people begin cheating their techniques and even their gear, to achieve a better score on their choreographed drill in the same way they would in a competitive environment. Another pitfall of the objective standard is that it might actually be demotivating; it may actually keep you from pushing yourself. If you achieve some arbitrary score, you may stop trying to get better.

Timers, scores and qualification drills can be very seductive. They allow you to celebrate your successes and measure linear improvement. Be careful you don't let them create a false sense of confidence or distract you from pushing yourself to your limits.

CHAPTER 26

RESPONSES, LEVELED UP!

CRITICAL INCIDENT DECISION MAKING

Get inside your
own head to thwart
the guy who wasn't
bright enough to
leave you alone.

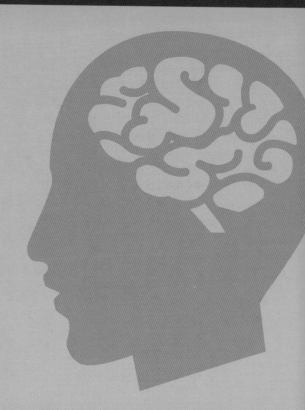

If you look at the history of the study of decision making during a combative moment, there is one revolutionary thinker who really stands out. His name is Col. John Boyd. Boyd described a decision making model called the "O.O.D.A. Loop." Although our industry regularly pronounces those initials as a two-syllable word "oo-da," a reliable source told me that Boyd referred to his theory as the "Oh-Oh-Dee-Ay Loop." As the guy who gets annoyed when my I.C.E. company, pronounced "Eye-See-Ee" Training Company, is referred to as "Ice" Training, I am going to endeavor to use the pronunciation of the initials from here on out!

Trivia out of the way, the letters stand for, "observe, orient, decide, and act." At its simplest, the O.O.D.A. Loop is a four-step process that describes your body perceiving and taking in data, focusing on it, making a decision about what to do with that information, the action you take as a result of that decision, and then the repetition of that sequence, the "loop."

Originally, the Loop was described for fighter pilots. Boyd was an instructor at the Red Flag exercises that pitted Air Force pilots against "adversaries" who were trained to simulate the maneuvers and tactics of enemy pilots. Boyd literally wrote the book on air combat maneuvers and plane-to-plane fighting. At one point in his career, he actually revolutionized that aspect of training for the U.S. Air Force. In that position, he described his O.O.D.A. Loop, and later refined it.

If you research the O.O.D.A. Loop, you'll see very quickly that it's not as simple as these four steps may seem at first glance. There are a lot of influences, there are a lot of feedback loops, there are decisions to be made going forward and backward to allow interpretation of the loop, and Boyd described it as a much more complex thing than most people in our firearms community tend think about it. The U.S. Air Force adopted that model and Boyd was invited to crossover from the Air Force to the Marine Corps. The Marine Corps then adopted the O.O.D.A. Loop as the starting point for their discussions about combative operations, and it eventually went from being something fighter pilots thought about in terms of sitting in the cockpits of their planes, all the way up to something generals and strategic planners would use to help their decision in theater-wide conflicts. It was then filtered down from the theater level all the way to the individual combatant in a fight.

An in-depth study of Boyd's own meanings and interpretations of the simple words that form O.O.D.A. reveal a complex and sometimes subtle process. For example, Boyd's explanations of what he meant by "orient" include references to one's beliefs, expectations, training, and plans. As it pertains to our discussion of armed home-defense, in Boyd's most thorough discussions of the O.O.D.A. Loop, there is definitely accounting for the kind of rapid decision-making and instinctive reaction we actually see in real dynamic critical incidents.

It has since then flipped to where, in the self-defense community, we often talk about Boyd's theorem only in terms of the bad guy's O.O.D.A. Loop. In fact, you'll often hear the statement, "Interrupt the bad guy's O.O.D.A. Loop," or "Get inside the bad guy's O.O.D.A. Loop" during shooting school instruction. Essentially, this means to do something that affects or interrupts the bad guy's plan of action. By doing this, you are making his actions less effective, because you are constantly resetting him back to the beginning of his course of action, resetting his Loop, by making him do things he has to adjust to based on his observations. I call that "combat efficiency," and it's a great way to think about your actions. Any action you take while you're in a fight should significantly affect the bad guy's ability to hurt you or whoever you're trying to protect.

One problem with the usual application of the O.O.D.A. cycle is that bad guys don't really go into brain lock when you step to the left or move in closer to them. All humans have natural reactions and the ability to apply learned techniques or quickly improvise intuitive responses when dealing with rapidly changing circumstances. The key to beating an opponent is to train your *learned responses* (as we've previously discussed) directly with the appropriate *learned stimulus*, so that you can force your opponent into an improvisational mode that will increase your chances of survival.

With all due respect to Col. Boyd and his explanations, I think the specific language of the O.O.D.A. Loop, based on what we know today about human decision making, non-cognitive decision making, learned stimulus response, and operant conditioning, is a bit cumbersome. I believe we need to move beyond Boyd's terminology, because it doesn't immediately account for either the power of recognition or the reality of reaction. Further, in some explanations, it over-complicates the collection and processing of information, as well as the filtering of options. In its most commonly provided explanations, it also misses the idea that you can experiment to see what works; and when you find out that something works, you can get a positive feeling from it and, in turn, repeat that technique to the point of an automated ability to perform it appropriately.

Let's walk through the development of your defensive shooting ability in an efficient training model.

You go out to the range, you keep both eyes open, you focus on your target, you drive the gun out kinesthetically, you get the hit, and you say to yourself, *That's awesome, that works, I'm going to keep doing that.* That is base-level intuitive defensive shooting.

Next, you make the target challenging enough that you are required to use your sights. You practice driving the gun out, you pick up your sights, align them, place them over your target, and maintain that sight picture while pressing the trigger. Again, you get the hit and think to yourself, *That's awesome, that works, I'm going to keep doing that.*

Next, you mix the two techniques together with the appropriate stimulus. You don't use your sights when you don't need to, and you do use them when the difficulty of the target requires it. You *learn* how to do things: you put the right stimulus in, process some information, and execute your learned response. There's a target—you don't care if it's 10, 15, or 20 feet away—your brain recognizes what to do, you do it, and you get the hit you need to get. Nowhere in there do you need to be aware of how far the target is, nowhere in there is there a complex decision of how fast you should pull the trigger (i.e., you're not thinking in terms of one quarter of a second, in one third of a second, or in one half of a second). There does not need to be a specific decision about whether or not to close an eye and focus on your front sight. Those complex decisions do not

COL. JOHN BOYD'S ORIGINAL O.O.D.A. LOOP

When being proactive or planning for how to deal with a future event that is relatively slow moving in nature, the traditional O.O.D.A. Loop serves us well.

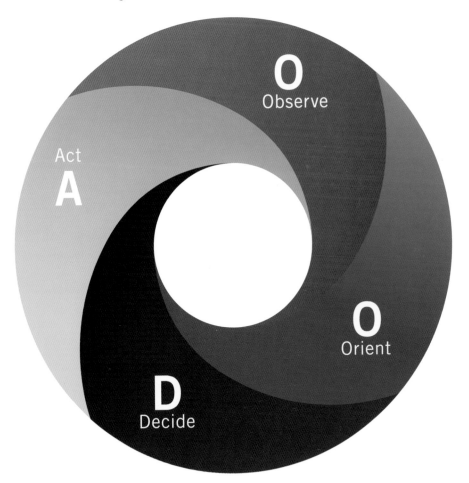

O
Observe

Act
A

O
Orient

D
Decide

need to happen if your training model is properly set up.

This is why I believe it is important to evolve the discussion of decision making under stress away from the more cumbersome model. Knowing what we know about neuroscience and human decision making, we can describe the process of learned actions, unlearned actions, and instinctive reactions in a better way.

O.O.D.A. EVOLVED

In the past, some people have, understandably, argued that the word "sense" would have been a better term to use than "observe," since the concept at hand addresses more than only physical vision. Indeed, the concept is less about sight and more about taking in information.

Information comes in through a variety of paths and your brain perceives whether you recognize it and whether you form memories. When the limbic system gets involved, you have reactions and/or responses. Hopefully, based on frequent and realistic training, you recognize what to do in a threatening situation, that your response is non-cognitive. You may recognize the situation as a threat and reach for your gun. I've heard many stories of people who have said they were in a threatening situation, they didn't even know what was happening, and all of a sudden the gun was in their hand and they were shooting. That's *recognition*; it's performing a learned skill as a *response*.

In this manner, the preferred Loop is going to be an O.R.R. Loop—"Observe, Recognize, Respond." It uses the information your body collects and takes advantage of all of the things that can happen, because of frequent and realistic training. You observe, you recognize what's going on from your training and visualization, and then you respond.

Once you're in the fight, again, you simply observe, recognize, and respond. You have to keep the act of *recognition* in the process—for instance, the bad guy has been hit and stopped, thus, your appropriate response would be to stop shooting—even though many people argue to cut that out and make the process automatic again, returning to the idea of observe and respond. In reality, you simply just can't do that. You cannot take a *learned response* and make it *instinctive and automatic*. Besides, I've already established and proven that you really wouldn't want to do it that way. You don't want to instinctively draw and fire and then recognize that you didn't need your gun. You *need* that non-cognitive decision making step.

There's been a lot of good research done on this concept in the last decade or so and, as a result, there are many good places you can get information on non-cognitive decision making, how powerful it is, and how it really affects every aspect of our lives—including the potential for survival during a dynamic critical incident. For those interested in understanding this facet of counter-ambush training at a deeper level, I recommend the books *Blink*, by Malcolm Gladwell, and *Gut Feelings*, by Gerd Gigerenzer. Gigerenzer is a German psychologist who has studied decision making, and he's considered an expert in the way the brain solves problems quickly. Gladwell is a very popular writer who has studied and written extensively on both the development of expertise and non-cognitive decision making.

Because I'm talking about all of this in the context of an ambush, I must also integrate the concept of natural reactions into the model. In Boyd's discussions, natural reactions were accounted for in his "Orient" phase. Because mental and physical focus are inherent in one's natural reactions to being surprised, and because they are the precursors to many other natural reactions during a lethal fight (changes in heart rate, blood flow, vision, hearing, etc.), I prefer to use the word "react" to cover this step in the cycle.

THE O.R.R. LOOP

The preferred Loop uses information collected and takes advantage of realistic training, when you are not caught off-gaurd.

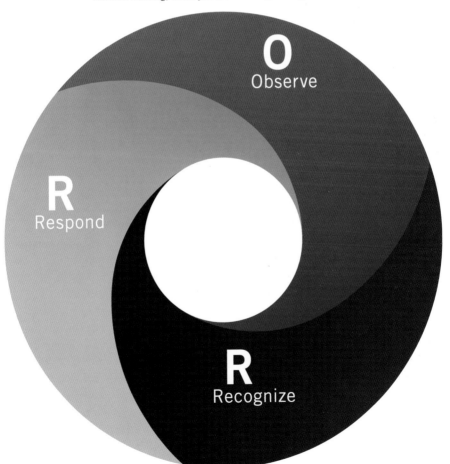

O
Observe

R
Respond

R
Recognize

For the appropriately trained person, the best Loop in an ambush situation, then, would be O.R.R.R. (O3R): "Observe, React, Recognize, Respond."

Observations consist of *all* the information you take in, not just what you see. A loud noise, the feeling of being grabbed, and all the other things your senses take in many times a second are all observations. It is observation that starts the cycle, of course. When it comes to creating stimulus/response patterns, however, you can't think of analyzing the data in the way most people do when they first think about an "observation." You need to keep in mind, especially when designing your training model and structuring your practice routines, that *tying the response to the appropriate stimulus is key.*

For instance, if the mechanics of a reload are practiced without the stimulus of live-fire slide lock, then, when the gun runs empty in an actual fight, the shooter is forced to cognitively analyze the failure and then (hopefully) recognize the situation calls for the response of a reload. If, instead, all training for the emergency reload starts with a realistic surprise—that is, one that's not staged—the shooter will be more likely to skip the time-consuming analytical step and proceed directly to the learned (practiced) response of reloading the gun.

This makes the whole process more efficient and shows the need for a keen appreciation of how non-cognitive observations—ones we don't need to process at a high level because of frequent exposure—can speed your response time. This also gets you back to the preferred

O.R.R. Loop: In the previous example, there's no need for an instinctive *reaction*, because the slide lock does not catch the well-trained shooter off-guard. Only someone who constantly topped off their gun in training and counted rounds to avoid slide-lock would be caught off-guard by its occurrence. (Before you laugh, keep in mind that, within my lifetime, the leaders in the private sector training industry taught that slide lock was to be *avoided* on the training range!)

Ultimately, you want to have a way that is trained and/or planned to respond to the threat, but you also have to accept that you may not. There are so many variables that cannot be predicted in a dynamic critical event such as a home invasion, you must be open to the idea of not having a response in place. After all, that is the ultimate premise of the counter-ambush training approach.

What do you get in the absence of recognition? You get an observation, your natural instinctive reaction, and then you improvise. *This is what happens in the absence of training.* You don't want to leave your life or the lives of your loved ones in the hands of untrained improvisation. You don't want to be making up what it is you need to do in the middle of your dynamic critical incident.

If your reload technique involved hitting the slide lock lever or the slide release to send the slide forward every single time you did a slide lock reload, but for whatever reason in your actual fight the slide ends up forward when you're reloading, you have to improvise. Maybe you've done a lot of malfunction drills, so you have a plan for what happens after you insert a magazine into your gun and go through your pattern of hitting the slide lock lever, but don't notice that it doesn't cause a round to be chambered. So you click, you tap, you rack (chambering a round), and then you can fight. That's two or three seconds you didn't need to waste in the middle of a fight. Or maybe you *do* observe that the slide is forward when you insert your new magazine, but you have no recognized response, so you have to *improvise* racking the slide—and, maybe, in that case, you lose only one second of precious time.

It all comes down to training as realistically as possible, using what you know about the most likely situations

THE O.R.R.R. (O3R) LOOP

For the well-trained, this is the best Loop in ambush situations.

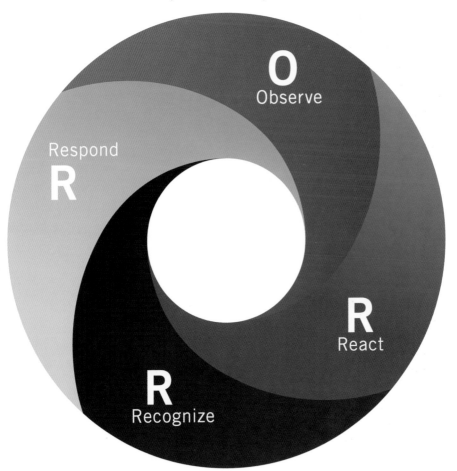

you could face. You must develop skills that make the most sense in your context, learn to recognize what's most likely to happen to you, and train to respond in the most efficient way possible so that you can defend yourself and others in a counter-ambush moment.

As I've just explained it, then, for the untrained or poorly trained person or for situations you simply haven't yet trained for, the decision making loop is O.R.I.: "Observe, React, Improvise." Still, and despite all the conversation so far, improvisation should not be seen as an automatic *fail* during the fight. In fact, many people who are untrained or whose training wasn't appropriate to the context of their fight (for instance,

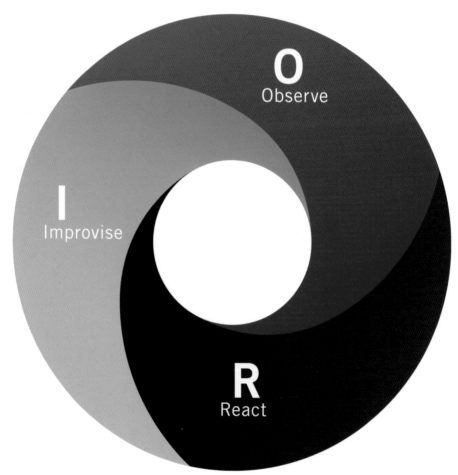

THE O.R.I. LOOP

Decision making Loop for the untrained or poorly trained person.

O Observe

I Improvise

R React

those who train to shoot in the Weaver position, but then improvise an isosceles stance response during an actual counter-ambush moment), often prevail. Humans are surprisingly good at improvisation, but we are *better* when we've trained realistically to respond efficiently.

Of course, you want to respond so efficiently (via O.R.R.R.) that you take your enemy out of their plan and so force *them* into an O.R.I. Loop that you can then defeat more easily. Looked at from another perspective, you want to make sure you have been planning, selecting gear, and training in a way that prevents you from being overwhelmed by cognitive and non-cognitive observations that you haven't trained for or can't cope with. Your goal is easily met through an efficient counter-ambush training model that incorporates training in *context*.

Context is a key component in capitalizing on everything that humans do well under stress. The biggest component of context, of course, is the presence of the stimulus that should be eliciting the trained response. To obsess over performance in isolation from the context of use misses the point of learning appropriate stimulus/response patterns. It is also important to remember that eliminating context from training often prevents people from choosing gear and techniques efficient for the broadest range of plausible circumstances. When reality interrupts the performance plan in a controlled environment, you are forced to fall back into improvisation.

Think about how this model fits into your observations of actual fights and how it relates to your training model. Are you depending on time to analyze and make a complex decision? Are you setting yourself up for O.R.R.R. or O.R.I.? Are you leaving stimulus/response out of your training?

Colonel John Boyd was a genius who bucked the system time and time again to help people understand his observations. Since he first proposed his O.O.D.A. method of looking at the problem, and though that method was geared toward a specific audience, it has been morphed, co-opted, and adjusted to fit a variety of contexts. There is no doubt that, when being proactive or even planning for how to deal with a future event that is relatively slow moving in nature (such as the land invasion of a country or a corporate takeover), the traditional O.O.D.A. Loop serves us well. In the context of counter-ambush training and dynamic, chaotic, lethal fights, integrating an emphasis on the power of recognition and focusing on stimulus/response patterns in your training is a natural, and necessary, evolution.

Mental Play— Imagining is Preparation

By Ken Murray,
Author of *Training at the Speed of Life*

I was just getting ready to leave town for the beginning of the long lap of the country I do once a year in support of my five-day, reality-based training (RBT) instructor schools. I pulled up to the gas pumps at a local filling station and began to fuel my vehicle. Within seconds of beginning the fueling process, a beat-up vehicle containing two nefarious looking characters came rumbling in beside me. The passenger came bouncing out of the car toward me, looking shiftily around. He had "the look"—you know exactly what I'm talking about, that predatory demeanor that caused every one of my alarm bells to go off.

I adjusted my position and put my hand near my hip, ready to draw and shoot this guy, if things went terribly wrong. I removed the gas nozzle from the fill spout of my car, aimed it directly at him, and told him to stop, as I shifted my gaze back and forth between him an his partner in the car. He stopped dead in his tracks with an audible "*Wha?!*" followed by a "Hey, brah, I just need a couple dolla's ta get me an' my man

down da road." I told him I wasn't an ATM and used a couple choice, directive expletives to help punctuate the fact that I was the inappropriate choice of the day for financial support.

He wheeled around, hopped into the car, and left without further discussion. Yet the incident didn't end there for me.

Now, I have no idea as to the true intentions of the passenger and his pal that day. Perhaps it was simply aggressive panhandling, perhaps it was the initial phase of a robbery or carjacking. I'll never know for sure, but once I was back in my vehicle, I continued to play the saga out in my head.

In my imagination, I saw the passenger who'd approach me reach into his waistband and pull out a pistol. As his movements telegraphed what was happening, I begin to move, while drawing my P7. Using my vehicle as a barrier, I quickly check the surroundings and move to a position that places the other few people in the parking lot out of the line of fire. I raise my weapon, confirm that he indeed has a gun, and I begin firing. There is no time or necessity for a verbal challenge. Six rounds zipper him, starting at the pelvis and moving up through the torso.

He crumples to the asphalt. I continue to adjust my position in anticipation of the second guy getting into the fight. I tactically reload my pistol, retaining the original partially expended magazine that was still holding three rounds.

I shout to the shocked observers to get down, while the suspect vehicle speeds off, leaving the initial perpetrator behind. I catch a partial plate number and mentally note the make, model, and direction of travel. I then yell to the witnesses to the event to stay back and to call 9-1-1, tell the operator that there has been a shooting of an armed robbery suspect, and tell them that the white guy in the red shirt behind the white SUV and trailer who's holding the pistol pointed at the guy on the ground is the robbery victim.

I keep my head in the game, checking my surroundings while keeping the shot suspect covered. The sheriff's department shows up remarkably fast, though not surprising, given that the police station is within sound of the gunshots. I identify myself and follow the directions of the responding deputies. I know exactly what I am going to say to them and, more importantly, what I am not going to say to them. I know who I am going to call. I know from studying the works of Alexis Artwohl and others that I will likely have some time and memory distortions of the event, despite the fact that everything seems crystal clear in my mind at the moment.

I know from studying the works of Lt. Col. Grossman that there might be some physiological effects to deal with, but that I have legally and morally done exactly the right thing.

The entire event is playing out just as I have rehearsed time and time again in my mind, a game of "What if?" as a means of crisis rehearsal. The entire mental rehearsal takes a mere five minutes out of my day, but it absolutely prepares me for how to respond to a real crisis in the event one ever happens.

I know the value of mental rehearsal during life-threatening events. While I have not tested its value in a gunfight, I have experienced the effects during a skydiving mishap, in which I had my first critical malfunction of my main parachute. The malfunction put me into a high-speed, disorienting, unrecoverable spin. It took me less than a second to make the decision to cut away my main chute and deploy my reserve. In fact, I can't even really call it a decision, but rather a reaction to the preparation that I had done. I was experiencing an event that would surely kill me, but I had mentally practiced on every ride up to jump altitude what to do in such an instance. Because of that, I performed the corrective action flawlessly and I enjoyed an exhilarating reserve parachute ride to the ground.

I contrast my parachute failure experience with that of a video I show in my instructor schools of a very experienced skydiver who has an identical malfunction. That skydiver, unfortunately, could not make the decision to cut away his main parachute. The video camera on his helmet captures his indecision in horrid detail, as he slams into the ground at high speed. He had approximately 30 seconds to make a life-saving decision, but, because he had neither the actual experience nor crisis rehearsal, he was incapable of making that simple cutaway decision. It cost him his life.

Reality-based training, or at least this form of it, doesn't require any equipment or a specialized facility. It is a journey of the mind. Dennis Waitley, author of *The Psychology of Winning*, describes the value of high-quality visualization. While working with NASA staff and Olympic athletes, Waitley used sophisticated equipment that recorded the brain and muscle firings of astronauts and athletes who were visualizing their own perfect performance in upcoming events—the

brain and body were reacting as though the visualized performance was real. This type of rehearsal has proven to provide a decisive advantage to those who use it.

Playing "What if?" and imagining yourself performing perfectly in critical incidents helps you prepare for critical encounters and can definitely provide you a decisive edge, when combat is upon you. Simply practicing skills will not necessarily prepare you for the totality of the fight. It might assist with winning the physical fight, but what about the other things you need to survive? Will you survive psychologically? Emotionally? Financially? Legally? Professionally? Socially? If not, and as Dave Grossman says in *On Combat*, you will be a one-shot disposable police officer—and that is unacceptable.

Crisis rehearsal is an extremely effective method of helping prepare for the entire fight, since you can, at your leisure, begin to go through the process of what you are going to say and do in the

THERE I WAS, FULLY PREPARED MENTALLY FOR A LETHAL FORCE ENCOUNTER, BUT I HAD BROKEN ONE OF THE MAJOR TENETS OF A WINNING A GUNFIGHT—BRING A GUN.

aftermath of a critical incident. Reading the great works on the subject by authors such as Dave Grossman, Alexis Artwohl, Bruce Siddle, Bill Lewinski, Dave Klinger, Brian Willis, Wes Doss, Gavin DeBecker, and certainly this book's author, Rob Pincus, among others, helps provide the grist for the mental mill. It is then up to you to put that information into mental practice on a regular basis. Turn events that have gone well into calls that go bad. What if that guy hadn't given up? What if the passenger had gotten out of the car to help out the guy you were arresting or had just shot? What if that had been a gun instead of a wallet that angry motorist went for so quickly in his glove compartment? Playing "What if?" and fixing problems before they occur in combat can provide you some amazing, cost-free feedback with which you can critique your own performance and so get better and better each time as you recognize your own shortcomings.

As for me, I sat there in my car that day gloating to myself at how flawlessly I had performed. I even reached back and patted my holster as a means of reassurance of the value that carrying a pistol in these violent times provides—and then I felt the blood drain from my head, as I discovered my pistol was not in my holster. It was, instead, at my feet in the car, since I had pulled it out prior to leaving the house and placed it there to make my long drive more comfortable, rather than having it poke me in the back all day in my waistband holster. Had things gone terribly wrong that day, my pistol, while only a few feet away, was not where I expected it to be, where I would have needed it to be. There I was, fully prepared mentally for a lethal force encounter, but I had broken one of the major tenets of a winning gunfight—bring a gun.

My mental rehearsal that day has since caused me to fix that major shortcoming. What shortcomings will your mental rehearsals reveal to you?

About the Author: Kenneth Murray is the Director of Training for the Armiger Police Training Institute, located in Florida's greater Orlando area. He has spent more than 20 years as a police and military trainer, specializing in the field of reality-based training. In the late 1980s, he cofounded SIMUNITION, and he has authored numerous articles and policy papers on the safe conduct of projectile-based simulation training exercises. Murray also taught the first instructor schools in North America on how to conduct safe and effective tactical simulations. Since that time, his training principles have been adopted by thousands of agencies, both nationally and internationally. In addition to the training programs taught through the Armiger Police Training Institute, he is an advisor to the Killology Research Group founded by Lt. Col. Dave Grossman, and along with Col. Grossman, he coauthored the entry dealing with behavioral psychology in the Encyclopedia of Violence, Peace and Conflict. Murray is also on the advisory committee of the Association of Defensive Shooting Instructors.

CHAPTER 27

COMBAT FOCUS® SHOOTING

From observation to innovation, the author and his
team of Combat Focus® Shooting instructors
took the haloed, textbook approach to
armed self-defense and turned it on its ear.
Welcome to the new era of surviving a lethal encounter.

There's been a lot of information provided to you in this book thus far. If you're an experienced shooter, some of it you may have heard about from other instructors, but I'll bet much of it may be at odds with what you already know (or think you know). Too, if you're new to shooting, much of this may be overwhelming. But, if you've gotten this far and are still with me, I think some background on how I arrived at the concepts in the book and the methods I teach regarding the issues of armed home-defense tactics is both prudent and pertinent, especially before you endeavor on these last few chapters dealing with shooting drills and mental training.

My Combat Focus® Shooting (CFS) program is an intuitive shooting program designed to help the student be more efficient in the context of a dynamic critical incident. The CFS program is the flagship program of I.C.E. Training Company and the cornerstone of all the firearms instruction I provide. CFS has a sister program called Dynamic Focus Shooting, which is taught by the same instructors and available as part of the curriculum at all Gander Mountain Academy locations around the United States.

Many people have asked me about the name over the years, sometimes bluntly asking how a guy who has never been in combat could possibly think that was a legitimate label. They have a point. The initial idea was that, in combat, you focus on the threat, and my instructors and I were primarily teaching people to focus on the threat while they were shooting.

At the time, I thought it was brilliant. As the years went by, though, I've often said I should've used "Dynamic Focus" as the primary name, as you tend to focus on the important stimuli during any dynamic event—and, in truth, we teach people to (dynamically) shift their focus to their sights when they need to in order to hit a more challenging target. Over the years, we have really used the names interchangeably for various audiences and contracts, but the brand has always been and will always be CFS.

CFS was first taught in the fall of 2003, at the Valhalla Training Center. To understand the early development and evolution of CFS, it is important to understand exactly what Valhalla Training Center (VTC) was.

When we first started teaching this course, it was much less of a program than it is now. Like many new schools, we didn't really have a curriculum of our own, just a collection of principles, techniques, drills, and concepts that were largely picked up along the way, often modified, and not very well organized.

It wasn't until 2004-'05 that CFS really started to look like what it is today. In 2003, it was just the name of a class. In fact, in the very first advertisements for VTC, it was listed as the "Combat Focus Technique," as part of our defensive pistol courses and recreational events. The story of how I ended up running Valhalla has been told many times before; suffice it to say it was a huge opportunity I wasn't going to pass up, but, if you had asked me in September 2002 if I would be running counter-ambush training for a full company of U.S. Special Forces soldiers in September

I.C.E.

INTEGRITY · CONSISTENCY · EFFICIENCY

TRAINING

2004 and certifying instructors assigned to Navy S.E.A.L. Qualification Training to teach my program little more than a year after that, I would've laughed at you. Heck, I didn't even have my own program to teach them!

To understand how it all happened, you have to understand what Valhalla Training Center was. VTC was a reality-based training center that, today, is no longer in operation, but it was a center I ran from 2003 until 2007. During its existence, it was recognized as one of the most advanced facilities in the world. It was even identified in a 400-plus-page white paper as the most advanced, private sector, close-quarters training facility available to the U.S. military. In addition to standard ranges, we had a 360-degree live-fire scenario and simulation area that allowed us to test the efficacy of our training programs and our students' abilities to apply the skills we were teaching them, in a realistic, emotionally powerful setting.

The scenario ranges featured reactive and interactive targets and sound and light effects, and they could be used for non-lethal scenario training with expert role players. While the focus was on personal-defense and high-level military special operations training (regular clients included U.S. Army Special Forces

and Naval Special Warfare units), we were also a sister company to a five star resort. That meant that we could literally have 50 to 60 Green Berets on property going through pre-deployment training in extreme close-quarters counter-ambush one day, and a team-building event for a multi-national company the next.

Though the opportunity to piggyback on the business of the resort by running training courses for civilians was part of the original business plan, the development of the programs for the military was unanticipated. In late 2003, I was contacted by members of 10th Group stationed at Ft. Carson, Colorado, who wanted to rent the facility to conduct their own training. This was a pivotal moment. Our business plan never called for renting out the facility, but I was particularly interested in overcoming some of the mistakes I'd seen made in military and law enforcement training. At the same time, the U.S. was at war in Iraq, and I didn't want to ignore the opportunity to support the efforts of our soldiers in their preparations for deployment overseas. I rolled the dice and told them that we didn't rent the training center, rather we provided training. When I did that, I challenged them to send a couple representatives to one of our Extreme Close Quarters Tactics (ECQT) courses,

which, at the time included a day of Combat Focus® Shooting and two days of combining unarmed combatives with contact shooting in the context of an ambush situation. I committed to them that if they did not find value in the program, I would reconsider renting them the center.

10th Group sent two respected members of their unit to the course, which I tailored to include dealing with what happens if a threat grabs the rifle of a soldier moving through a building and needs to be dealt with via unarmed techniques and/or a pistol. Ultimately, the unit made the decision to take advantage of the unique close-quarters training we offered.

In addition to the ECQT program, our package integrated traditional drills, Special Forces Advanced Urban Combat

(SFAUC) training, convoy security training, and a variety of other components. Ultimately, I was running a five-day, 18-hour package we called "Extreme Close Quarters Counter Ambush," and it is some of the work of which I am most proud.

At the core of those training weeks were the principles that were CFS. During the week, every soldier participated in at least four hours of CFS range training with their pistol and rifle. Overwhelmingly, the feedback we got on the value of the CFS approach was very positive. I cannot accurately articulate the pride I felt when I first heard a Special Forces officer state that the training we had conducted would undoubtedly save lives in an upcoming deployment. Still, that was surpassed by the feeling I got when the first Green Beret, upon his

Back in the day, we didn't believe that unsighted shooting, that old "shoot from the hip" way that looks so cool in those old westerns and gangster movies, had much real-world application in a true fight for your life. Things have changed.

return stateside, told me the training *had* saved lives.

That type of training became the real focus of VTC for the majority of the time it was operating. On non-training days, we also had a fair number of resort guests who took the opportunity to have a "recreational experience" at the facility. That recreational experience, often their first time shooting a handgun, became an outstanding research opportunity for me as a teacher and program developer.

I had long been frustrated with the status quo in defensive firearms training.

The author, far right, guiding students through a home-defense long gun class.

So much was my frustration that, while I sought out as many learning opportunities as I could, had attended classes, and had picked the brains of the leaders in the industry, I was concurrently developing my own ideas and approaches based on the observation of actual defensive shootings, the behavior of people in training scenarios, and research into how the brain and body work together under the stress of a fight. In fact, as early as the mid-1990s, I was working to develop a more efficient approach to defensive shooting.

At the time, I'd had the great fortune to meet and work with Hector Martinez, a United States Marine with experience in the first Gulf War, who was teaching at the Protective Services school at Ft. McClellan, Alabama. He was an innovative trainer, with a passion for making things as realistic as possible for those going through the PSD School, where he covered weapons and tactics. Marty and I spent many hundreds of hours on a variety of ranges over the years. In fact, it was Marty who originally developed the Figure 8 Drill (covered later), for teaching realistic counter-ambush responses to protection teams. He was also the first instructor to indoctrinate me to into using the command "Up!" on live-fire ranges. Eventually, Marty took a job teaching at FLETC (Federal Law Enforcement Training Center) and, unfortunately, we lost him too soon, but the influence he had on the way I teach can clearly and still be seen today.

I entered the firearms industry in the late 1990s and, while still working in law enforcement, began teaching on my own or for various companies and writing for industry magazines. In 2001, I got my first green light to write about absolutely whatever I wanted in a national publication; *S.W.A.T. Magazine* gave me my own column, and I penned an article entitled "Qualification Isn't Training," in which I condemned quite a few common practices and advocated a few potential improvements for the reader who wanted to draw a stronger correlation between their performance during training and practice sessions and their ability to apply their skills in a real fight.

Like I said, that was 2001. Even then, though, it was clear to many of us in the industry that many of the things that had been taught in defensive handgun courses during the preceding few decades were way off. The advent of the dashboard camera era in law enforcement and the increasingly frequent use of high-quality security cameras was revealing a huge disparity between the range and competition successes of the "Modern

"DEFENSE WITH A HANDGUN IS *THE* AMERICAN MARTIAL ART."
—LT. COL. GROSSMAN

Technique" versus performance during actual defensive shootings. What was most compelling was that, despite 30-plus years of dogmatic teaching by many excellent instructors and academies, there was no evidence showing that the techniques being taught were actually being used on the street. This meant that those forced to suddenly defend themselves from violence were, essentially, improvising their techniques.

What we were seeing in the videos looked nothing like what we were seeing on the training ranges. Observations in reality-based scenario training, which involved high-level simulation (as we were doing at VTC) or role players and training guns that used marking cartridges, were revealing how these improvisations came to be. Around the same time, I was heavily influenced by Tony Blauer and his research on the importance of understanding how the body's natural reactions to being attacked must be integrated into unarmed training, in order to increase efficiency. In that world, martial artists had long been criticized for the fact that few of its choreographed and flowery techniques were ever used in actual personal-defense events. As best-selling author (and authority on the combat mindset) Lt. Col. Grossman has said, "Defense with a handgun is *the* American martial art." That made me realize we were doing the same thing on our side of the fence.

Our "martial art," defense with a handgun, was full of overly mechanical, highly choreographed theory that only worked well at the range-dojo. Reality-based training (then still a very young part of the industry), and actual reality

(via the more and more common video-taped shootings), were showing us what we needed to do. I began to change the way I taught, and my approach to teaching defensive shooting was becoming a lot more about emulating and refining what people were doing in the *absence* of training or in spite of poor training during actual fights, and a lot less about traditional target shooting and the things that help people perform well on objectively scored range drills. In fact, in my first book, I said that CFS was more *recognized* than developed.

That gets us back to VTC and our recreational clients. Over the years, I was pushing the envelope of teaching people to develop defensive shooting skills more efficiently. In the 1990s, I became a big believer in unsighted shooting for the majority of defensive situations; relatively quickly, I would work that into my courses. But, I was still starting off my students with sighted fire. Except for use in some extreme close-quarters situations, I avoided the term "point shooting," and I never believed it was a good idea to teach shooting "from the hip" via a partially extended position. Sure, I explained, this looked great in 1950s gangster movies, it didn't seem to make much sense in a gun fight. Indeed, "point shooting" was already a toxic term in professional circles, one that meant far too many things. We believed that partially extended positions were hampered in their effectiveness, as they were only effective across a very narrow set of circumstances and they generally left the gun unsupported and unprotected from threats within arms' reach.

I now teach to either keep the gun in close (as covered in the section on extreme close-quarters shooting) or extend it fully. By extending the gun fully into your line of sight, you can align the gun in the same way you align your finger when you point or use any other device that relies on hand-eye coordination. But, back in the early 1990s, even the most progressive instructors who believed in the efficacy of unsighted fire at extension in close quarters were still teaching sighted fire first. The conventional wisdom was that you had to teach sighted fire to establish good shooting fundamentals. Only then could you responsibly teach unsighted fire to a defensive shooting student.

I vividly remember a conversation I had with Harry Humphries, then the Director of GSGI and one of the founding members of S.E.A.L. Team VI, in the early 2000s. In that conversation, he assured me that while he and other top-end military personnel, and people like me who shoot (at the time) tens of thousands of rounds a year, could certainly get their hits in defensive shooting circumstances without the use of sights, novice shooters absolutely needed to be taught "the

basics" first—and, by "basics," he, of course, meant sighted fire. When a guy like Harry says something like that, you tend to believe him. I have no doubt that he absolutely believed it to be true, plus it's always nice to hear that you are somehow in the same league as an elite Navy S.E.A.L. (even if he was just being gracious). But, with all that said and all we've learned since, the recreational clientele at VTC allowed me to prove that the necessity of starting out students with "the basics" of sighted fire simply wasn't valid.

When a student comes to me for life-and-death skill development, I am only so willing to "experiment" with the process. There is no way I can teach something in a defensive shooting class that I *don't* know to be effective. Similarly, there is only so much experimentation you can do with an experienced shooter, because they already bring so much with them to the experiment. Most instructors and schools in the past have only used their own cadre of instructors (or trusted, experienced students), to develop new drills and attempt to push into fresh ways of developing skills. But the truth is, only an irresponsible, "mad

Teaching to shoot with sighted fire first was considered part of "the basics." Even top-level military professionals believed that was the way. Following the advent of the era of security cams and law enforcement dashboard recordings, we now know that teaching unsighted fire is just as valid as teaching sighted—maybe more.

scientist" approach would allow one to take real students and risk not letting them develop skills in a proven system. Not only is that potentially dangerous, it is disingenuous. Let's not forget that the student is paying me for what he or she believes is the best information I have to keep them alive. The *recreational* client, however, is another thing entirely. If they leave without any extra holes and a smile on their face, our relationship was a success, and while I was working with them, I could push the limit of experimentation, as long as we were being safe.

The staff of VTC and I employed a more and more stripped down training process, before taking recreational shooters through "the maze." The maze was what we called the 360-degree live-fire shoot house. This building, originally designed by Tom Forman (the owner of VTC) to be a recreational facility, was approximately 16,000 square feet of fake public and private spaces, all surrounded by a steal box. We would take the shooters into the maze, which encompassed two floors with more than two-dozen halls and rooms, and walk behind them as they made their way through with a handgun held in the High Compressed Ready position. Our instructions to the students were very simple: "If you see a threat target, shoot it until it goes away or goes down."

In the maze, two types of targets were used, mannequins that dropped on hinges, and motion sensor-triggered pop-out targets that were exposed for about two seconds. All the targets were at distances between about eight and 20 feet. Generally, the mannequins would require two to five chest shots before going down,

that number of shots depending on their exact placement, the speed at which the shots were made, and the specific setting of the hinge.

Eventually, our standard drill evolved to provide the students a safety presentation first and then let them fire about 15 rounds at a chest-sized target 12 feet away, before taking them into the maze—and we *never* teach them to use their sights. In fact, because originally we were using guns from the training inventory, we experimented with some that didn't even have sights. These were full-size 9mm personal-defense guns, exactly the kind of gun used by most police officers and chosen by people serious about personal-defense.

We ran our students through three drills: "Extend, Touch, Press"(two to four rounds), "Up!" (two to four rounds), and "Multiple Shot Up!" (the remaining rounds in the magazine), all of which you will read about later in this book That was it. We taught them, in about one minute, how to stand and how to hold the gun, gave them less than 10 minutes of live-fire practice with those 15 rounds fired, then took them into shooting simulations that were more realistic than most police and military personnel ever get (and at a level hardly any CCW permit holder will ever approach). The end result? Our students succeeded. In fact, they did *amazingly* well.

Quickly, the results of these experiments turned the way we taught sighted and unsighted fire head over heels for good. There was no more doubt left in my mind: the fundamental defensive shooting skill was *unsighted fire*. Sighted fire was (and still is) taught by us as an

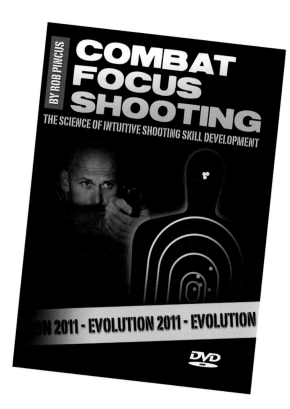

There have been two editions of the Combat Focus® Shooting book published. The Combat Focus® Shooting DVD was released in 2011.

advanced skill to be used when higher levels of control are needed.

In addition to the many hundreds of recreational shooters having no experience at all, we also naturally had our share of experienced shooting enthusiasts come to VTC. When we had those more advanced students, we would sometimes see stark contrast in the ability of them to apply their skills in the maze. We would frequently see people who were very used to shooting on a target range or in choreographed competition fail to even engage at all the surprise targets exposed for those two-second periods. All too often, the experienced student of the traditional approach to defensive shooting would "double-tap"—fire two very fast shots at a target and then stop—at

a mannequin and then turn away, *even though the threat was still there.* They simply hadn't absorbed and were unable to follow the same simple direction our novices were given: Shoot until the target goes down or goes away. Of course, those are the exact instructions I would give you if you needed to shoot an actual threat in your home!

I knew I was on the right track in changing my teaching methods when I started seeing this disparity in my student shooters, but it wasn't until I had run that experiment hundreds of times that I was ready to tell the world that we in the shooting industry had been getting some really important things wrong. It was then that I was just about ready to start writing books about and doing instructor development for this new "Combat Focus® Shooting" program.

The evolution in this kind of teaching, for me, was happening fast, but it wasn't until we got the request from Navy Special Warfare S.E.A.L. Qualification Training (NSW SQT), in late 2005 (after they had gone through the end-user course), to certify a group of their cadre as instructors in the CFS program, that it set in just how important the work we were doing really had become. Of course, there were some missteps along the way and some things that didn't prove to be useful during the experimentation. I also had to let go of many assumptions and concepts that I had long trusted. One thing I quickly found out was that this process was about the *students*—it couldn't be about what *I* did or could do—and I learned that the fundamental concepts and drills had to apply to *all* students, not just the extremes of the best or the worst.

I certainly didn't have all the answers when I started—I still don't!—nor did I come to the conclusions on my own while sitting at a desk trying to reinvent the wheel. Ultimately, the program was developed with the help of some outstanding instructors who weren't afraid to take everything they had learned, turn it sideways, shake it, mix in a ton of new information, throw away a lot of what they had previously believed, and trust in the evidence we were getting back from our observations and experiments. CFS owes much of its existence to Brad Schuppan (NRA and law enforcement), Jeremiah Miles (Naval Special Warfare; NSW), and John Brown (NSW), who worked with me at VTC. Also owed credit are the guys inside the elite military units who weren't afraid to look outside the box for training, and the leaders in civilian law enforcement like Sheriff Bill Masters, San Miguel County, Colorado, who were ready to change the status quo. Ultimately, a huge chunk of appreciation needs to go to Tom Forman for letting us rework, rebuild, repurpose and, basically, have our way with his creation, the laboratory that was Valhalla Training Center.

Today, Combat Focus® Shooting is an intuitive shooting program, which means, as we've discussed throughout this book, that it is designed to work well with what the body does naturally. Combat Focus® Shooting is designed to make the shooter more efficient; it is not focused merely on learning to hit targets. We know that you need to learn hit targets with as little time, effort, and energy expenditure as possible. In that manner, Combat Focus® Shooting is designed to work well in the context of a dynamic critical incident. CFS is not a program that will make you a great marksman or help you win competitions; it is designed to help you survive an unexpected fight during which you need to use a gun to defend yourself or others.

What you are about to read next are the core components of the Combat Focus® Shooting program as we teach them today. They are the fundamentals you need to master in order to be prepared to defend yourself and your family inside your home with a firearm.

CHAPTER 28

PRACTICE DRILLS:

THE COMBAT FOCUS® SHOOTING WAY

It's not IDPA or IPSC, and it's not shooting for bull's-eye score or against some arbitrary time par. This is about taking your gun handling skills off the range and putting them into real preparation for the thing you hope never happens.

was asked by a student in a class of instructor candidates, whether the basic Combat Focus® Shooting course outline assumed its students already had a basic knowledge of shooting fundamentals. The student who posed the question, Dan Pauley, is an accomplished instructor of both tactics and martial arts and was serving as a sergeant with the Telluride Marshal's Office. The Marshal's office is the primary law enforcement agency in Telluride, Colorado, and a sister agency to the San Miguel County Sheriff's Office, where I serve as a Training Officer. Although I knew that Dan, a long-time police officer and pistol enthusiast, was asking about such things as sight alignment and sight picture, I responded with the fundamentals of shooting as I saw them.

"The fundamentals of shooting are, look at the target, extend, touch, and press."

Dan, who had been training with me at the Valhalla Training Center as part of a recurring tactical refresher program with his agency for about three years prior to attending this particular instructor development class, understood completely. He was certified as an instructor during that class and now integrates Combat Focus® fundamentals and concepts into his training. A major part of his and any Combat Focus® Shooting Instructor's integration is the use of specific drills performed with shooters of all skill levels, to help them develop a good understanding of their personal balance of speed and precision. Many of these drills I'm now presenting here, for you to utilize on your own or with others.

Contrary to some rumors, Combat Focus® Shooting is not an unsighted shooting program, but it does emphasize that shooters need to understand when and when not to use the sights. Running the fundamental drills as they are meant to allows the acquisition of that knowledge and skill set to happen in a very efficient way. (Of course, the best way to ensure you're getting the proper experience with these drills is to attend a training program with a certified Combat Focus® Shooting Instructor!) For example, the Extend, Touch, Press! and the Up! drills need to be set up so that shooters engage a target area realistically simulating the high center chest area of a human at a distance of eight to 10 feet. I've yet to see a student who couldn't consistently get hits under those conditions with unsighted fire.

After you have developed a comfort with both unsighted and sighted fire, you will begin the process of developing an intuitive recognition of which is the best choice under a given circumstance. The first step in that development is, of course, shooting under a variety of conditions (the more realistic the better), so that you can experience for yourself what your personal balance of speed and precision is for any number of given circumstances. An instructor cannot answer the "at what distance/size/situation should I use my sights," with any answer other than "When you need them." Understanding when that is requires realistic training and is part of being a Warrior Expert.

The balance of speed and precision drills are great places to start creating templates for your Warrior Expert mind. While participating in any of these drills,

In the context of home-defense, you might very well find yourself surprised and having to shoot from your couch or a chair. The only way to become efficient at this is to practice realistically.

remember the tenets of safety, comfort and competency!

THE EXTEND, TOUCH, PRESS AND THE UP! DRILLS

The most basic, fundamental drills in Combat Focus Shooting are the "Extend, Touch, Press" (ETP) and the "Up!" drills. You should have derived from reading the book this far that what I and my instructors teach is that the basics of defensive shooting are not about firearms terminology, weapons maintenance, stance, the law, or most of the other things students are sometimes taught prior to actually putting holes in paper. So, in order to prioritize focus for many people, I pose the following question: "What would you teach someone you know and cared about if you had only 30 seconds to prepare them for the use of a loaded gun against a lethal threat?" Your answer would be "The fundamentals of defensive shooting," but my answer is, "Look at the target, extend the gun to parallel with your line of sight, touch the trigger, then press the trigger repeatedly until the threat stops." I have found that, with a little critical thinking, most people agree with this answer.

The two drills I'm covering in this chapter drive that point home for all shooters, everyone from the newest to the most experienced. Starting with the ETP drill, the only goal is to impart to the shooter an understanding of the three separate steps of final presentation towards the target and the firing of a round. Through this drill, you can achieve and practice proper trigger control, grip, and presentation. You want to

Pointing is one of the most basic human abilities, and it is best done in your line of sight. Therefore, the most intuitive position from which to shoot a firearm is in and parallel with the line of sight toward your threat.

make sure your stance is consistent with a plausible position during a dynamic critical incident (lowered center of gravity, weight forward, generally squared off towards the target, etc., as I've already discussed).

Using this drill as a warm-up, with another shooter acting as range officer, is a great idea. When doing so, it is imperative that shooters hold their shots until the "Press" command in order to get the most out of the drill. Do not be tempted to just go ahead and shoot on your own. Here's how the drill goes.

The ETP drill is performed at a realistic critical incident distance from the target—nine to 12 feet is a good place to practice most defensive shooting drills (though I'll have more to say about training distances in a bit). Now, here's how the overall ETP drill should be performed in its entirety. As you go through this very simple but important drill, keep in mind that, when I and my instructors teach this, we give three separate commands, one for each step.

1. EXTEND: The first step in basic defensive shooting is extending the firearm *in and parallel with* your line of sight to the threat. Since you'll be working with a target set at the nine- to 12-foot range, remember to focus on the target, not any

part of the gun, but keep the gun in your line of sight. You'll probably find pretty quickly that you can lower the gun out of your line of sight and still achieve dynamically accurate hits, but doing so would be counterproductive; consistency is paramount. Keep the gun in the same place relative to your head, where you would want it if you were to need to focus on your sights, should the need for precision increase.

Remember that the act of reaching towards something—to pick up a drinking glass on the counter, for instance—places your hand in your line of sight to that object. At a young age, a special awareness of the cause and effect relationship develops, and the action of reaching turns into pointing. Pointing is one of the most basic human abilities, and it is best done in your line of sight. Therefore, the most intuitive position from which to shoot a firearm is *in and parallel with* the line of sight towards your threat.

2. TOUCH THE TRIGGER: Yes, you're going to want to press the trigger, and that will happen in quick succession to touching the trigger once the flow of this drill becomes intuitive. But, when you first engage in this kind of drill as defensive training, you first must separate touch the trigger from press the trigger. Doing so lessens the amount of deviation from the intended point of impact after you do press the trigger. This is, initially, about trigger control, which is probably the one consistently required mechanical portion of all shooting endeavors that doesn't have a natural corollary

3. PRESS THE TRIGGER/MAKE THE SHOT:

For most students, developing a feel for the three steps of ETP drill doesn't take much time. I and my instructors, working first to get our students into a good defensive position and then moving through the three steps, routinely have our students making combat-accurate hits in just a few shots.

Some things to look for as you initially work through this drill. If your handgun is moving after extension and before the shot, you are not presenting the gun properly and/or you are probably looking at the gun or sights. In most cases where a shooter moves the gun around after it is fully extended, it's because they are looking at the gun.

Be sure not to "cheat yourself." The truth is that, at the pace you will be moving, there is no penalty in efficiency for looking at the sights, and they do increase accuracy potential. This is why it is very important to stress that all hits in the accepted combat-accurate area are equal at the beginning of the drill. As the realism of the conditions and the pacing increase, you'll be more interested in shooting faster, so you will want to have established comfort with the concept of unsighted fire by then.

After you are consistently getting dynamically accurate hits with ETP, you should switch to one single command. I usually use the word "Up!" which is how

ETP DRILL
1 EXTEND
2 TOUCH
3 PRESS

the drill got its name, for all three actions. During Up! drills, make sure you are not pausing between steps, rather you should be letting extend, touch, and press all run together to eventually become one fluid set of movements. Be sure, too, to reach full extension before the first shot breaks, as this will allow you to build on a stable foundation for the multiple shot strings that you'll start practicing soon. Know that when you first transition to Up! drills and the command is given (or you think it to yourself), you might even go slower than you did during ETP the first

Training is how you learn and improve your skills. After that, you need to practice often enough to maintain them.

few times. This is natural, until you feel comfortable speeding up.

After a few repetitions of the Up! drill, you will be ready for Multiple-Shot Up! drills, in which you vary your strings of fire from two to five shots. It is likely you will be firing more than one shot in order to stop a threat inside of your home, so you should practice multiple shot strings of fire.

TRAINING DISTANCES

When you get ready to practice your shooting, as someone interested in home-

defense, you have a bit of an advantage over the average person who carries a gun in the public space: You can predict the distances at which you may need to shoot with a much higher level of reliability. Well, at least you can reasonably know the maximum distance *and* predict the most likely distance based on your planned barricade areas. If you plan to barricade in your bedroom, for instance, you can measure the distance from your planned barricade position to the door, and then you know your most likely shooting distance. You can also figure the furthest distance inside your home (the furthest *practical* distance, given movement, angles, and possible positions of human bodies), and use that as a basis for the practical limit of your practice, as well. Certainly, you could always develop your ability to shoot at further distances, but you should focus on the most likely distances first. As a defensive shooter, you already know you are most likely to be shooting at a chest-sized target and have a head-sized target as your alternate area. Given these fixed limits, the geometry of your training and practice should so be limited (again, initially, and in the context of home-defense practice, not practice for bull's-eye score or a speed shooting competition).

As you develop your skills, keep in mind that distance and size are *independent* variables. You cannot interchange them by shooting at smaller targets at closer distances in order to simulate a larger target further away. It may seem like you could, and this is sometime taught, but determining the *perceived*

surface area of a target doesn't work that way. I'd been taught it did and used to believe in the practice, but, after trying to make those cheats work with actual students, I can tell you it doesn't.

For some reason, people are much more affected by distance than they are by size. When you are practicing to shoot chest-sized targets at 15 feet, you should use chest-sized targets at 15 feet, and not a target half that size at 7½ feet. Also, don't fall for the idea that you should train on a target smaller than you actually want to (or have to) shoot. When you do that, you run the risk of learning to shoot at the wrong pace or even using the wrong techniques. For example, most shooters don't need their sights to hit a chest-sized target at 12 feet. If you decided, though, to try to shoot at four-inch targets at that distance all the time (the belief being so that you could be "better" than you need to be), you might *need* your sights, which slows you down, and you end up learning the wrong thing as it applies to training for armed home-defense. So

ditch the better-than-you-need-to-be practices and take advantage of the opportunity you have as someone preparing for home-defense to be able to train more specifically for exactly what you may need to do.

THE BALANCE OF SPEED AND PRECISION DRILLS (BOS&P)

The BoS&P drills are the heart of intuitive shooting skill development. Any drill that has at least two commands and could require at least two different sets of motor skills be demonstrated (based on the fundamentals of the need for the balance of speed and precision and the required application of this skill), is a BoS&P Drill.

The idea with BoS&P drills is to impart variables so that you must use a cognitive process to determine which motor skills need to be executed. Remember, in the real fight, there *must* be a cognitive process to determine what you need to do. Specifically as it regards to shooting, the thinking part of your brain must rec-

AS A DEFENSIVE SHOOTER, YOU ALREADY KNOW YOU ARE MOST LIKELY TO BE SHOOTING AT A CHEST-SIZED TARGET. GIVEN THAT, THE GEOMETRY OF YOUR TRAINING SHOULD SO BE LIMITED.

ognize how much skill you must apply to get the hit you need. This determination cannot be made until after the threat is recognized.

The problem is that, on the practice range, if you are standing in front of a target waiting for a signal to start your string of fire, you cut the cognitive process out of the loop. You *know* how this goes. Picture yourself in front of a photo-realistic or silhouette-type target. As you wait for a command to fire or the tone from a beeper, you may not realize it, but the thinking part of your brain has already primed your motor cortex to perform the exact motions necessary to hit the target. Your brain is already priming the muscles and, so, when the tone goes off, you execute the motor skills without any real decision making.

Because decision making is so important and because you want to develop skills in context, you need to respond during BoS&P drills to a variety of stimuli, so that you can determine exactly what physical execution you need. In this manner, drills that involve multiple potential targets and multiple potential commands to fire are what define Balance of Speed & Precision drills (and the good news is that the design of the targets, number of targets, or the commands you use are virtually unlimited).

If you understand these principles, then some paper, a couple cans of spray paint, and at least one training partner are all you really need to create a vast array of BoS&P drills—and, as long as your setup follows the plausibility principle it pertains to target size and distance, they are *all* worth doing!

THE S-E-B DRILL

The S-E-B Drill is named after a target created by the Law Enforcement Target Company. This target has two large boxes and a triangle inside the gray, bowling pin-shaped silhouette, along with a series of small shapes containing the numbers one through six spaced around it. The large square in the high center chest area represents the combat-accurate hit area. In the S-E-B drill, it is best to have a training partner to issue commands.

Of course, if you do not have access to these specific targets, you can still run this drill. This is one of the reasons we have begun referring to this drill as the "Basic Balance of Speed & Precision" drill. As you would expect, what is important is the concept of the drill, not exactly what the target looks like.

The person calling commands should alternate calls between "Up!" and one of the numbers on the target, "Two!" for example. The shapes surrounding the six numbers are significantly smaller than the box in the chest area of the target, so the shooter will get to experience the difference in the speed with which they can get consistent hits, at the given distance, between two differently sized targets.

There does exist the factor of predictability of slowing the shooter's response to the smaller, numbered targets. The effect of this factor is increased if the "Up!" command is called significantly more often (twice as often or more) than a number. If you're reading this before running the drill yourself, of course, the behaviorally surprising element will be somewhat lost, but you

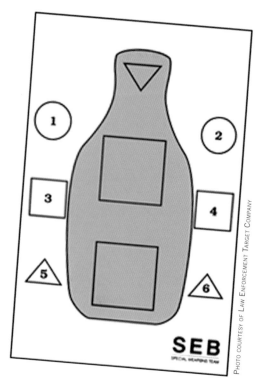

The S-E-B target created by the Law Enforcement Target Company is the primary target the instructors at CFS prefer to use. Instructors designate the large square in the high center chest area as representing the combat-accurate hit area.

should still practice more of the high center chest engagements than you do the smaller target areas.

Extremely tight groups in the chest area might be applauded on the target range, but, from the CFS perspective, they probably indicate that a shooter is shooting too slowly.

Some things to look for when working through this drill. Some shooters will have a tendency to try to shoot the smaller, less predictable targets as fast as they shoot the large box. If you are consistently missing, you should slow down. On the other hand, if you are consistently hitting but shooting at the same speed, you can probably hit the *center* box faster!

APPS AND ADVANCED BOS&P DRILLS

In the Spring of 2010, Boxkite Media and I created an application that can be loaded onto various devices (beginning with Apple's iPhone, iPod, and iPad), that lets the user customize a menu of possible commands, in order to simulate being on the range with a training partner who understands the concept of the BoS&P drills. The folks at Boxkite Syndicate are my long-time trusted web gurus, and the principals of the company have both been through Combat Focus® Shooting

The Combat Focus® Shooting app lets the user customize a menu of possible commands to simulate being on the range with a training partner who understands BoS&P drills.

courses. The app randomizes the commands selected from options to match the targets being used. Information can be found online through the I.C.E. Training Company website (www.icetraining.us). The app is a huge advantage for those interested in training themselves to tie their shooting skill to a cognitive decision.

In 2011, the CFS team worked with the Law Enforcement Target Company to develop our own target, item number CFS-BSP. This target takes the company's SEB target that we talked about earlier to the next level and is even more versatile. It features a gray silhouette with a lighter gray, high center chest rectangle,

a properly oriented triangle in the head (upside down, to represent the "soft" area of the face from the outside of the eyes to the center of the mouth), and six small numbered circles around the outside. These circled numbers are also colored blue, yellow, or red. In addition, there are two large black squares, marked A and B, underneath the silhouette. This gives you *three* chest-sized target areas, seven head-sized, a complete upper torso and head, and at least five different target colors, all on one target. This, in turn, gives you an almost limitless number of commands you could use to initiate shooting. Some examples:

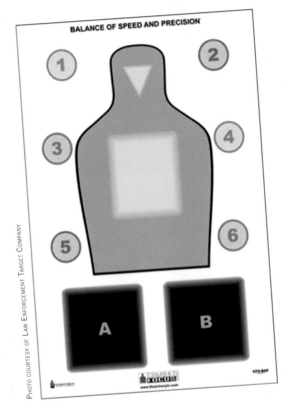

In 2011, the CFS team worked with the Law Enforcement Target Company to develop its own target, item number CFS-BSP. This target takes the Law Enforcement Company's SEB target to the next level and is even more versatile.

- **UP!** (for the chest)

- **A!** (for multiple shots in the lower left box)

- **FIVE!** (for a single shot at the circle containing the 5)

- **RED-LEFT!** (for a single shot at the circle containing the 3)

- **20 MINUS 15!** (for a single shot at the 5)

- **CHEST** (for multiple shots at the chest rectangle)

The idea, of course, is to mix this up with the help of a partner. By keeping the scenario as unpredictable as possible, you will be better prepared for whatever comes down the pike in a real life.

CHAPTER 29

TRAINING RESOURCES

To be ready to face the thing you hope never happens to you requires gear, money, training, and a host of other resources—including the one that ties them all together.

arlier in the book, I mentioned the idea that we all have limited training resources. It should be pretty obvious to you that, regardless your knowledge, interest, lifestyle, budget, needs, occupation or location, there are limits to the amount, type, and intensity of defensive training you can do. Let's discuss the most important training resources and how managing them affects your ability to properly train for personal-defense.

MONEY

It would be disingenuous to insinuate that having a significant training budget won't make your training better. Having a bigger budget increases your access to equipment, venues, and coaching. In some ways, having a big pile of money might also free up more training time. Regardless, when it comes time to spend that budget, you need to do some research and spend your dollars wisely. Just because you can afford a course, doesn't mean it's worth attending, and just because you can afford a new training tool that got high marks in a magazine review doesn't mean it will really be beneficial for you. Just as importantly, you should realize that you don't need to have a large training budget to have a very good training program. Can't afford fancy targets? Old cardboard and spray paint can work wonders. Can't afford expensive training courses? You can buy books and DVDs, access free training material on the Internet, and even interact with many instructors through social networking sites.

VENUE

One of the most frequent questions I get from my own students is, "How can I practice at my range, which doesn't allow rapid fire/holster work/movement/people targets/etc.?" Having access to a range (formal or informal), where you can actually practice appropriate

TRAINING RESOURCES ARE ALWAYS LIMITED. YOU HAVE TO DO THE BEST YOU CAN WITH THE RESOURCES YOU CAN JUSTIFY.

defensive shooting techniques is *incredibly* important for high-level skill development. This is one of those resources for which there really isn't an easy way around. All the dry-fire, slow-fire, from-the-table-fire in the world won't help you learn to manage recoil control at the highest levels of speed under the most likely shooting circumstances.

That said, you can practice your presentations from the holster to the ready position at home with a dry gun and get 100-percent value. You can then practice shooting from the ready position, including a rapid string of fire, on those ranges that won't allow holster work. As a final step, you could add laser trainer to your dry-fire practice and get reps in from the holster to the shooting position with real accountability for your first shot.

Unarmed defensive and even scenario training for threat management can likewise benefit from this type of approach. You don't have to be at a formal dojo to train in unarmed skills and you don't need to be at a world-class training school with well-trained role players to get some value out of scenario training. While a proper training venue is important and should be utilized when you can both find and afford one, a creative person can work around virtually any limitation, at least for practice between sessions at a good venue.

EQUIPMENT

At first, many people think of equipment issues as a budget issue. How many cool training toys can they afford?

Fancy targets, reactive targets, interactive targets, laser systems, timers—you name a defensive shooting skill and there is probably a gizmo someone is selling to help you train to it. I say buyer beware. As I've already noted, just because you have a lot of money doesn't mean you need to spend it.

Quite often, people overthink their training equipment. Simply put, when it comes to defensive shooting, once you have allotted some time, bought a firearm with a good holster, a few extra magazines, a good supply of ammunition, and gotten access to a range, you don't need much more. As I've said, you can get a lot done with simple targets, a can of spray paint, and a good training partner. When it comes to unarmed defensive training, the same is true. A decent venue and a motivated partner will go a long way, even without fancy simulated weapons or training suits. Don't let a lack of bells and whistles in your training environment be a stumbling block to training realistically.

COACHING

After time, I think coaching is going to be the most important training resource you can cultivate. Keep in mind that when I say "coaching," I'm not just talking about a person standing on the range or someone on a mat who's walking you through a new skill or critiquing your performance.

The first thing a coach gives you is knowledge, but that knowledge can be gathered in a variety of ways. Yes, having an in-person experience during a formal training class is probably best. But, books, articles, online blogs, discussion forums, training DVDs, and various other resources are also available to you. Of course, you need to use critical thinking and discretion when taking advice from any expert and via any method, and, yes, the further away you get from a face to face experience, the harder it may be to judge someone's value or expertise. This is where much of today's social media and discussion forums can be helpful. Personally, I answer dozens of e-mails and private messages every week from people I've never met and who are seeking all types of advice and answers on gun use for personal-defense.

Is a formal school just simply out of your budget for the foreseeable future? Then the performance critique you would otherwise get from a coach at that big-budget school could come from a home-town training partner who knows what to look for (perhaps having been through a course himself), and you can even find ways to critique yourself, via the review of still pictures and/or video of your training sessions.

MOTIVATION

This last training resource is one that you, by demonstration of your reading this book, already have at an above-average level. Most people won't even think to prepare for personal-defense—and, of those who do, most will stop at acquiring their equipment. Only a small number of truly motivated people will actually seek out the training and perform the practice necessary to develop reasonable skills in preparation for the worst-case scenario. What I would suggest to you is to keep two things in mind as you move forward.

First, don't mistake enthusiasm for training for motivation to train. Training can be fun, and many people attend training classes as a hobby. Some even consider a course a year with their buddies as an annual vacation. But, in the interest of armed home-defense, don't be a hobbyist. Sure, it's great if you gain pleasure from knowing you are better able to defend yourself or your family if you need to. But, if the only reason you train is because you enjoy the training, you will inevitably start compromising that training. How? You'll start deferring to techniques you perform best in the training environment, rather than the ones best suited for dynamic critical incidents. You'll also start rationalizing the deficits of gear that you like, instead of choosing gear that is best suited to your context of personal-defense. Too, get bit by the training bug hard enough, and you'll start attending training courses without regard for the consistency or integrity of the material, instead using them simply to add another certificate to your collection.

Second, keep a training log. In 2008, I published *The Training Log Book*. It was a hardcover book with essays from more than 30 active instructors providing training advice to those interested in personal-defense. The second half of the book was filled with pages that had many areas to be filled out as you completed your training. These areas highlighted lessons learned, techniques, tactics, classmates, instructors, and areas for improvement after the class. I have found personally that nothing motivates me to train more than looking such notes and data. Every time I recall how much I learned during a course or practice session, it motivates me to want to go out and do it again.

TIME

I saved the issue of time to prepare and train for last, but it is probably the most important training resource I can think of, for it is that time you allocate for the preparation for personal-defense that most limits your ability to train. We can all find ways to compensate for a lack of any other resource, but,

without the allocation of some amount of time, all those other recourses are useless.

Of course, you don't have to have large blocks of time to make those resources work. In fact, many skill development experts would suggest that frequent short training sessions are actually better than long ones separated (especially when those long sessions are separated by long periods of time with no training at all). Taking that kind of approach, of frequently setting aside small periods of time to practice, whether it be dry-fire, live-fire, in-house scenario rehearsal, or any other training you see as necessary to securing your home and personal safety, is certainly one in line with how most of us lead our hectic lives these days.

The First Next Step

Now that you have read this book, you should form a plan. Before you put this book down, write down what your first "next step" will be and set a date for action. It doesn't have to be a terribly time consuming or expensive project. Any step is a positive one in the right direction. Maybe you're going to talk to your family. Maybe you'll upgrade your locks and doors. Maybe you'll sign up for a defensive shooting class. It really doesn't matter what you do, do something.

Let this page serve as your motivator and become a record of your commitment to taking action. I can tell you that I am sometimes a bit embarrassed when I find that I personally am not taking all the simple steps that I professionally advise others to take. Life is a busy thing, and many of us have the best intentions, yet fail to take action. Commit to some action right here and right now:

NEXT STEP:

_____

_____

_____

_____

Then document you successful completion of that step:

DATE TO BE COMPLETED: _____

How bad will both of us feel if there is a tragedy in your home, you weren't prepared for it, and yet this book is in the crime scene photos? Put this information to use. Knowledge is the foundation for your plans. You now have the knowledge—so go make the plan!

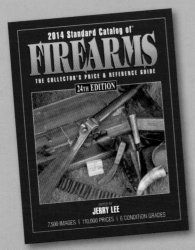

2014 Standard Catalog of®
FIREARMS
THE COLLECTOR'S PRICE & REFERENCE GUIDE
24TH EDITION

EDITED BY
JERRY LEE

7,500 IMAGES | 110,000 PRICES | 6 CONDITION GRADES

MASTERING
THE ART OF
LONG-RANGE
SHOOTING

WAYNE VAN ZWOLL

Gun Digest® Books
An imprint of F+W Media, Inc.

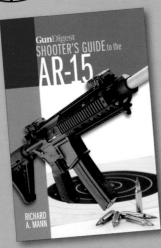

GunDigest
SHOOTER'S GUIDE to the
AR-15

RICHARD
A. MANN

HANDGUN TRAINING
FOR PERSONAL PROTECTION

How To
Choose & Use
The Best Sights,
Lights, Lasers
& Ammunition

Richard A. Mann

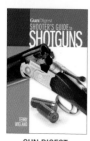

GUN DIGEST
SHOOTERS GUIDE TO
SHOTGUNS
U2146 • $19.99

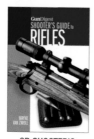

GD SHOOTER'S
GUIDE TO RIFLES
V6631 • $19.99

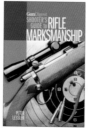

GUN DIGEST SHOOTER'S
GUIDE TO RIFLE
MARKSMANSHIP
U2928 • $19.99

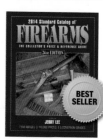

2014
STANDARD CATALOG
OF FIREARMS
U5072 • $42.99

GUN DIGEST
2014
U2618 • $34.

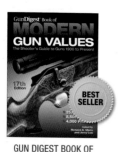

GUN DIGEST BOOK OF
MODERN GUN VALUES
U5559 • $34.99

GD BOOK OF THE
REMINGTON 870
V8197 • $32.99

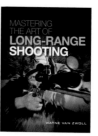

MASTERING THE ART OF
LONG-RANGE SHOOTING
U2148 • $29.99

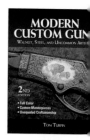

MODERN
CUSTOM GUNS
U3979 • $59.99

ABCS OF
RIFLE SHOOTING
U8579 • $27.99

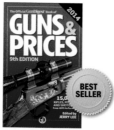

THE OFFICIAL GUN DIGEST BOOK
OF GUNS & PRICES 2014
(APRIL 2014)
U8735 • $25.99

GUN DIGEST 2015
(AUGUST 2014)
U8734 • $34.99

GUN SAFETY IN THE HO
(MARCH 2014)
T0031 • $15.99

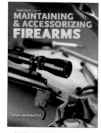

GUN DIGEST GUIDE TO
MAINTAINING &
ACCESSORIZING FIREARMS
(JULY 2014)
T0033 • $32.99

GUN DIGEST SHOOTER'S
GUIDE TO THE AR-15
(JUNE 2014)
U7713 • $19.99

GUN DIGEST GUIDE TO
MODERN SHOTGUNNING
(AUGUST 2014)
U9369 • $32.99

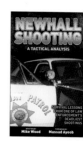

NEWHALL SHOOTING
A TACTICAL ANALYSIS
T1794 • $24.99

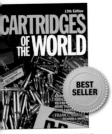

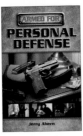

RTRIDGES OF THE WORLD,
13TH EDITION
V0801 • $34.99

ARMED FOR
PERSONAL DEFENSE
Z9404 • $19.99

COMPLETE GUIDE
TO 3-GUN COMPETITION
W6536 • $27.99

GUN DIGEST BOOK
OF THE .22 RIFLE
Z8581 • $19.99

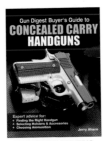

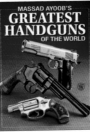

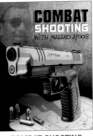

DGUN TRAINING FOR
SONAL PROTECTION
U2147 • $21.99

GLOCK DECONTRUCTED
V9707 • $29.99

GD BOOK OF
CONCEALED CARRY,
2ND EDITION
V9337 • $27.99

GUN DIGEST
BIG FAT BOOK
OF THE .45 ACP
Z4204 • $24.99

PERSONAL DEFENSE
FOR WOMEN
Z5057 • $22.99

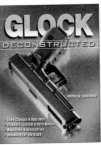

1911
IE FIRST 100 YEARS
Z7019 • $32.99

GUN DIGEST BUYER'S
GUIDE TO CONCEALED
CARRY HANDGUNS
Z8905 • $24.99

MASSAD AYOOB'S
GREATEST HANDGUNS
OF THE WORLD
Z6495 • $27.99

COMBAT SHOOTING
WITH MASSAD AYOOD
W1983 • $24.99

GUN DIGEST BOOK
OF COMBAT GUNNERY
Z0880 • $24.99

DEFENSIVE
NDGUNS SKILLS
8883 • $16.99

TACTICAL
PISTOL SHOOTING
Z5954 • $24.99

GUN DIGEST BOOK
OF THE REVOLVER
W1576 • $22.99

GUN DIGEST BOOK
OF THE GLOCK
Z1926 • $27.99

GUN DIGEST
SHOOTER'S GUIDE TO
HANDGUN
MARKSMANSHIP
U3674 • $19.99

CONCEALED CARRY
FOR WOMEN
U3668 • $22.99

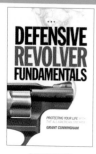

DEFENSIVE
REVOLVER
FUNDAMENTALS
U4713 • $22.99

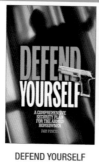

DEFEND YOURSELF
(MAY 2014)
U7396 • $24.99

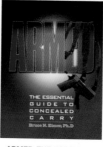

ARMED-THE ESSENTIAL
GUIDE TO
CONCEALED CARRY
W7927 • $24.99

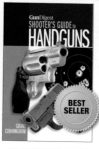

GD SHOOTERS GUIDE
TO HANDGUNS
V9633 • $19.99

GUN DIGEST
SHOOTERS GUIDE
TO THE 1911
Y0048 • $19.9

BIG-BORE REVOLVERS
W5866 • $27.99

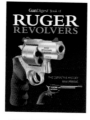

GUN DIGEST BOOK
OF RUGER REVOLVERS
U5073 • $32.99

MASSAD AYOOB'S
GREATEST HANDGUNS
OF THE WORLD, V2
W6538 • $27.99

THE GUN DIGEST BOOK
OF SIG-SAUER
(JUNE 2014)
U8736 • $32.99

HANDBOOK OF MOD
PERCUSSION REVOLV
U8580 • $24.99

GUN DIGEST BOOK
OF SURVIVAL GUNS
U1060 • $24.99

BUILD THE PERFECT
SURVIVAL KIT
U6487 • $18.99

LIVING READY POCKET
MANUAL: FIRST AID
U8353 • $12.99

FOOD STORAGE FOR
SELF-SUFFICIENCY
AND SURVIVAL
(MAY 2014)
U8352 • $17.99

BUILD THE PERFECT
BUG OUT VEHICLE
(JULY 2014)
U7403 • $17.99

THE UNOFFICIAL HUNGER
GAMES WILDERNESS
SURVIVAL GUIDE
U1956 • $17.99

PREPPER'S GUIDE TO
SURVIVING NATURAL
DISASTERS
U3133 • $21.99

SURVIVAL SKILLS
YOU NEED
W1803 • $22.99

BUILD THE PERFECT
BUG-OUT BAG
W6554 • $16.99

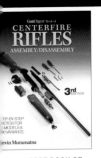

GUN DIGEST BOOK OF
'ERFIRE RIFLES ASSEMBLY/
DISASSEMBLY 3RD ED.
U2620 • $34.99

GD BOOK OF SHOTGUNS
ASSEM/DISSASEM,
3RD ED.
V6630 • $36.99

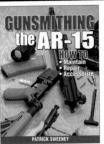

GUNSMITHING
THE AR-15
Z6613 • $27.99

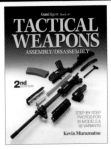

GUN DIGEST BOOK OF
TACTICAL WEAPONS
ASSEMBLY/DISASSEMBLY
U3671 • $29.99

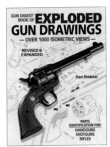

GUN DIGEST BOOK
OF EXPLODED
GUN DRAWINGS
Y0047 • $37.99

GUN DIGEST BOOK
OF REVOLVERS
ASSEMBLY/DISASSEMBLY
Y0773 • $34.99

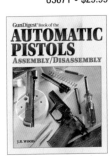

GUN DIGEST BOOK
OF AUTOMATIC PISTOL
ASSEMBLY / DISSASEMBLY
W7933 • $39.99

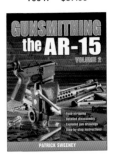

GUNSMITHING: THE AR-15
(MARCH 2014)
Z6613 • $27.99

CUSTOMIZE THE
RUGER 10/22
NGRTT • $29.99

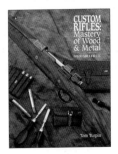

CUSTOM RIFLES:
MASTERY OF WOOD & METAL
V8196 • $59.99

GUNSMITHING:
PISTOLS & REVOLVERS
Z5056 • $29.99

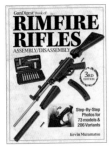

GUN DIGEST BOOK
OF RIMFIRE RIFLES
ASSEMBLY/DISASSEMBLY
W1577 • $34.99

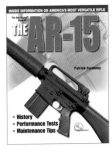

GUN DIGEST BOOK
OF THE AR-15
GDAR • $27.99

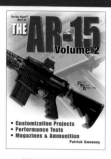

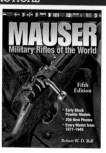

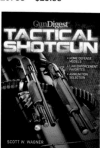
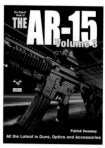
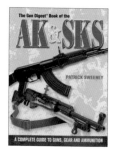

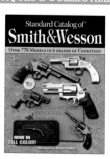
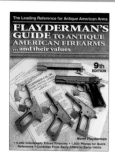
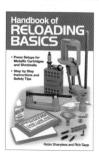
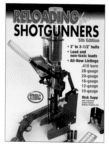
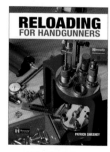
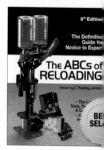

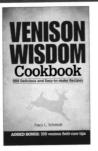

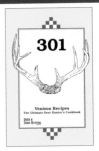

SPORTING CHEF'S
BETTER VENISON
COOKBOOK
Z1948 • $24.99

COOKING GAME
U2929 • $9.99

VENISON WISDOM
COOKBOOK
Z8928 • $14.99

WE KILL IT
WE GRILL IT
V6707 • $9.99

301
VENISON RECIPES
VR01 • $10.95

ADVENTURE
BOWHUNTER
Z9708 • $34.99

HUNTING MATURE
WHITETAILS
THE LAKOSKY WAY
W4542 • $29.99

DEER & DEER
HUNTING'S GUIDE
TO BETTER
BOW HUNTING
V6706 • $9.99

STRATEGIES FOR
WHITETAILS
WTLDD • $24.99

TOM DOKKEN'S
ADVANCED RETRIEVER
TRAINING
U1863 • $22.99

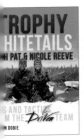

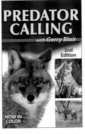

TROPHY WHITETAILS WITH
PAT AND NICOLE REEVE
(MARCH 2014)
U3680 • $31.99

LEGENDARY
WHITETAILS
W7618 • $29.99

GUT IT. CUT IT. COOK IT.
Z5014 • $24.99

PREDATOR CALLING
WITH GERRY BLAIR
Z0740 • $19.99

THE RUT HUNTERS
U7573 • $31.99

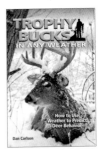

GAME COOKERY
U7125 • $24.99

THE MOUNTAIN MAN
COOKBOOK
U9370 • $12.99

TOM DOKKEN'S
RETRIEVER TRAINING
Z3235 • $19.99

TROPHY BUCKS
IN ANY WEATHER
Z1781 • $21.99